# Executive Protection: The Essentials

Terry Hipp

# DEDICATION

This book is dedicated to the men and women
who serve to protect others.

# CONTENTS

# ACKNOWLEDGMENTS

Years ago I attended a week-long training session that was supposed to teach me how to quantitatively and scientifically assess risk. This training was being presented by Sandia National Laboratories; a well-known and well-respected company that develops science based technologies supporting national security. They had developed a Community Vulnerability Assessment Methodology (CVAM) designed to be a risk-assessment tool using scientific methodology for making entire communities more resistant to terrorism. Having studied other Vulnerability Assessments and having attended several other courses about assessing risk, I figured this was going to be great training.

Throughout this training we learned how to apply principles by practicing in large public arenas and government facilities within the major metropolitan area this course was being held. I distinctly recall the instructors encouraging me to put a team of people together that could assist me in completing these types of assessments for a fee; suggesting that I could probably charge about 10K per assessment.

Within a year of attending this training I had the opportunity to use their methodology to assess risk for a large organization that had three separate locations. It took me almost a full year to complete it. This was partially due to the fact that I had other contracts I was working on at the same time, but also because the Sandia methodology was complex. By the time I was finished that year-long assessment I knew two things for sure. I would never use it again. I would develop something the average person could understand when completing an assessment that would determine risk. Some of Sandia's methodology is great if you are a scientist, but great methodology does not always align well with the average person's brain.

Ultimately, the information presented in this book has been influenced by experiences like these. Over the years I began to develop my own style and methods simply because they made sense to me. I am constantly looking for common denominators that regular people can effectively use to solve complex problems.

As such, I want to give thanks to every victim I ever interviewed; to every professor and instructor who taught me; to every expert who took time to answer questions over a cup of coffee and to every mentor who had enough interest to take me under their wing for a while. They have given me more than I could have ever imagined and I am quite sure they have all had some impact on this book.

# FOREWORD

There may be references in the book to gender neutral people, such as "the Principal" or "the Asset" or "the Executive". Obviously, those words may be substituted with the words "him" or "her". Likewise, "him" or "her" may be referring to an Executive. Although this book refers to the "Executive", the principles that are presented are applicable to a VIP, Celebrity, Politician and other people who need or want this type of protection.

Additionally, this book refers to the Asset primarily as a person. However, the primary principles covered in this book can be applied to a thing, a system, a building, an event or any other critical Asset. If you are considering a career in the Executive Protection field you are strongly encouraged to successfully complete some type of self-defense, martial arts or personal protection course. You should also consider completing a Handgun/Pistol/Weapons course before participating in any Executive Protection detail. These types of courses provide the foundational physical psychomotor skills required to provide adequate protection in the event of an emergency. More information about how to choose these courses can be found at AssaultPrevention.Org

There are no footnotes or endnotes in this book. There is no bibliography. If you are reading the eBook version there are hyperlinks to sources that are cited. If you are reading a print copy of this book there is ample information within the material cited to discoverable sources.

There are a number of statistics in this book. Statistics change frequently and I am sure that some of the statistics will have changed between the time this book was written and the time it gets into your hands. I encourage you to "look through" the statistics to the underlying points or principles that those statistics are representing.

There is really nothing new here. It is packaged and presented with my own unique view as to what I believe is important in the world of Executive Protection. I have been teaching these principles for many years with tremendous feedback from people who have attended my courses. These students were very diverse in their backgrounds, previous training, skill sets and professions – but the outcome of attending the courses are usually the same - Excellence.

The driving force to publish this book was two-fold. First, I have been repeatedly approached by other professionals to become involved in constructing an Executive Protection Course that would actually focus on the realities of Executive Protection; many books and courses do not. Throughout my career I attended more training courses than I want to remember that were filled with fluff and filler. Too much of what they spent my time on was stuff that was really cool but also very impractical and disconnected to the realities of Executive Protection.

Secondly, those courses had extraordinary price tags associated with them. Some instructors are simply taking the money that mostly fantasy-fueled testosterone is willing to part with through carefully crafted marketing plans in an effort to line their own pockets. For the curious person considering a career in Executive Protection, this book will NOT cost you thousands of dollars nor will it require you to sacrifice years of your time to figure out what the real-deal is.

Your paid delivery of the <u>Executive Protection: The Essentials</u> grants you a non-transferable license to retain a physical or electronic copy for personal use in your home or business. You may not create duplicate copies or excerpts thereof, whether electronic or printed on paper, for sale or distribution.

The author has done his best to provide accurate and up-to-date information in this document, but cannot guarantee that the information will fit your particular situation. These are copyrighted materials.

**A Final Note**
At the end of each chapter you will find a "Taking It To The Next Level" section. The suggestions you read there are, of course, completely optional. They are intended to give the reader who might be considering Executive Protection as a profession, some practical things to do that EP Agents often perform as part of their work. These suggestions will further your understanding of Executive Protection work in the real world.

This book was written in such a manner that it puts you, the reader, in the position of an Executive Protection Administrator who is ultimately responsible for a major protection event. As such, this book does not focus on tactical formations, emergency vehicle responses, complex extractions or firearms because once you understand the big picture of Executive Protection; those other things tend to fall into place on their own.

# 1

# EXECUTIVE PROTECTION TRAINING: MACHISMO, MIRAGES, MYTHS AND MONEY

A quick internet search using the words, "Executive Protection Training" reveals a number of courses that are available for about $250-$500 dollars a day. Add this to the air fare, meals and lodging and you have easily spent thousands of dollars to attend this type of training. The websites that offer this training look slick, with professional rotating pictures of limousines, private jets, yachts, limos and guys with guns. It is testosterone heaven. But wait.....there's more!

As you click through the tabs you see all the services that are offered: Personal Protection, Witness Protection, Dignitary Protection, Investigations of all types, and a multitude of courses that are offered - from Handgun Training to High Risk Environments. And, if you register for a course now, you get a 10% discount on your next outrageously priced course! With all of these great pictures and all these services that are offered, they must be legitimate and professional, right? Buyer, beware! Many of these websites are more like the Wizard of Oz than the Fantastic Four; because what lies behind the curtain is often a big disappointment. But you wouldn't know that from looking at those websites.

What motivates a man or woman to give an unknown organization thousands of dollars to attend training for a position they will probably never have?

## Machismo

The Spanish and Portuguese roots of this word have to do with masculinity being superior to femininity. Machismo, as commonly interpreted today in the United States is defined as a "strong or exaggerated sense of masculinity stressing attributes such as physical courage, virility and aggressiveness; an exaggerated sense of strength or toughness". This definition would describe the stereotypical perception many people have of the Executive Protection Agent or Bodyguard. In fact, these personalities are drawn to the profession. There are other reasons as well.

Author Bron B. Ingoldsby presented a paper at the Annual Meeting of the National Council on Family Relations in 1985 entitled; "A Theory for the Development of Machismo". It examines machismo. "Two characteristics dominant in the study of machismo are aggressiveness and hyper-sexuality. A biological model of machismo asserts that males everywhere tend to be more aggressive than females, a sex difference which appears to have a genetic base. A generally accepted psychological theory views machismo as an expression of an inferiority complex."

From this pool of people, we would expect to see men and women enlisting in professions like Executive Protection because they are driven by an inferiority complex and overcompensate by entering a dangerous profession, which in turn helps them feel superior. I can assert this is true. The bulk of my business is training, and I have probably trained several thousand students at this point in my career. One of the courses I teach is Executive Safety & Vulnerability. Albeit a small percentage, I have met my fair share of overcompensating students trying to deal with some psychological or physical inadequacy.

"Why do Boys and Girls Prefer Different Toys", is an article published in Psychology Today. Satoshi Kanazawa, an evolutionary psychologist at LSE is credited. An excerpt from this article: "Throughout the world, boys and girls prefer to play with different types of toys. Boys typically like to play with cars and trucks, while girls typically choose to play with dolls. Why is this? Growing scientific evidence suggests that boys' and girls' toy preferences may have a biological origin." In their studies "male rhesus monkeys show strong and significant preference for the masculine toys. Female rhesus monkeys show preference for the feminine toys, but the difference in their preference is not statistically significant". This makes sense, since most of the attendees of Executive Protection training are men. It is genetic.

Peter Langman, Ph.D., is Clinical Director at the national children's crisis charity KidsPeace and the author of Why Kids Kill: Inside the Minds of School Shooters. He wrote an article published in Psychology Today; "The Career Aspiration of Shooters". From that article: "The pattern of thwarted careers in law enforcement and/or the military can be found among serial killers and school shooters, as well as at least one spree killer." He goes on to suggest that some mass shooters have an interest in law enforcement and military careers in an attempt to bolster their fragile manhood. Kind of sounds like a recurring theme, doesn't it? Feeling inferior but acting superior equals machismo.

Gavin de Becker, in his terrific book, The Gift of Fear; "We trust security guards—you know, the employment pool that gave us the Son of Sam killer, the assassin of John Lennon, the Hillside Strangler, and more arsonists and rapists than you have time to read about. Has the security industry earned your confidence?"

LTC (RET) Dave Grossman's article; "On Sheep, Wolves & Sheepdogs" asserts the following:
- Most people are not violent. These are the sheep.
- Wolves are the bad guys and they prey on the sheep.
- The Sheepdog lives to protect the flock and confront the wolf.

Sheepdogs are people who run toward trouble, not away from it. They are the real deal, and thank God we have them. They are the good guys. They are also part of the pool that attends Executive Protection training. I like these people and respect them. Some have disposable income. Some get the tuition for these courses paid by their employer. However, not everyone is wired as a Sheepdog and even among those who are, there are a great many who lack training.

Ultimately we find a percentage of people attending Executive Protection courses questionable because they are enrolling for the wrong reasons. They want to work in an industry where there are varying degrees of force authorized, including firearms. A certain percentage of them are attending because they are driven by some deep-seated psychological need to overcome their own perceived inadequacies. Scary.

This is one reason why observers of the private security industry are critical of it. The industry recruits giant, human slabs of meat that cannot spell their names without help, and give them the professional title of Executive Protection Agent, Bodyguard or Security Guard.

How does the industry reduce the number of questionable people attending their training?

Part of the solution is for vendors who provide training to tighten up their screening procedures, which will never happen. Tightening up screening procedures would not be a great business model and will bring in as much money.

Perhaps applicants should be required to submit to some type of psychological exam or personality testing. How about an oral interview on the phone? A background check? There are several instruments readily available which would provide the vendor some minimal information about the mental and emotional state of a prospective student. Society would be far better off, and so would the security industry at large.

Why? Think about it. Statistically, it is much more likely that an Executive Protection Agent will use his mouth and brain rather than pulling out a firearm, much less pull the trigger. Yet, the majority of Executive Protection training traditionally focuses on physical skills, including firearms. Law Enforcement has paved the way in this respect. Law Enforcement requires their officers to qualify regularly with their firearms, but not their brains. There is really no effort made to determine if a student (or officer) possesses a sound mind. Security, Law Enforcement, Corrections and paramilitary organizations would benefit from more stringent screening.

**Mirages**
Perception is everything. Perception precedes thought. Thought precedes impulse. Impulse drives behavior. Smart marketing professionals know what neuromarketing is. In the context of a sales pitch, emotions come first. Those feelings can exert a powerful influence over the way we process any factual information that follows. In other words, if I can move your emotions, I can affect your decision-making. Look again at the pool of potential attendees already mentioned. How can I move them emotionally toward attending one of my courses? Look at a few of these Executive Protection training websites and you will quickly determine how that is done.

The people who provide Executive Protection training are in the business to make money. Often, the instructors are talented ex-law enforcement, secret service and military people who specialize in various aspects of training. Many of them are the real deal. I know my fair share of instructors across the country from attending their courses when I was early in my career. Becoming a vendor, speaking at conferences and providing professional training and consultation has given me ample opportunity to meet, evaluate and discuss training with a great number of them.

A quick glance at one of these Executive Protection websites leaves the potential student with the perception that they are dealing with a large organization; including staff in many cities that are extremely well qualified and educated, possessing the necessary experience to provide them with "certified" training so they can enter the field of Executive Protection. The disappointing reality behind the smoke and mirrors is some guy sitting in a basement somewhere working on that website.

A certification is simply a set of standards that must be met, and these companies are free to set their own standards. There is no national board oversight on standards in the Executive Protection industry. But the word, "certification", affects your perception. I use that word with my company training, but I also publish the standards we use that drive certification, so a prospective student knows up front how we design our courses. I also have the people who work with me listed as Key Players, because they are. Each one of them lends something important to my company and has for a long time. The photography I use on my company website is a combination of stock photography and pictures taken from the work we perform. It is entirely up to me, the CEO, as to the degree of integrity and honesty I will require the website to reflect to you; the consumer.

In contrast, the website you look at for Executive Protection training may be a gross exaggeration. The certification may be close to meaningless. The organization may be one or a few people. The backgrounds of the instructors may be exaggerated. It might be nothing more than a mirage.

**Myths & Money**

Written about with some frequency by others, many prospective students' perception of the Executive Protection Agent comes from movies and the media. This leads them to believe that they will be rubbing shoulders with the rich and famous while getting paid six-figures a year. Or that on their down-time they will be lying by the pool with Hollywood-esque babes who are wearing the latest lingerie from Victoria's Secret. Bodyguard and Executive Protection schools know this and they take advantage of it by taking money from people who are willing to pay thousands of dollars in order to fulfill an imaginary fantasy of protecting someone important.

Let me be clear. There is some excellent training available by some well-qualified instructors. But there is also a lot of Executive Protection training created by people who have had little or no experience around real-life threat or violence. I personally know a number of them. They have held positions in which they may have had the opportunity to protect a Celebrity or two, or perhaps an Executive. But they have never been under the stress of a real confrontation. What you learn from them is something theoretical that they learned from someone else who probably had no real experience either.

Essentially, they are public relations and marketing wizards looking for an opportunistic way to capitalize on what is primarily a male fantasy.

## The Real World

The need for Executive Protection is based on individual circumstances. Most executive threat in the United States comes from extortion based on sexual infidelity, stalking or burglary; and in these cases the Executive's need for a good attorney and a home alarm system far outweighs their need for an Executive Protection Agent. Rarely do we hear about an Executive kidnapping or attack in the United States, and you would be hard-pressed to find examples of Executive Protections Agents using any type of force, much less pulling a firearm or other weapon out in the line-of-duty. This is reinforced through the compendium in Gavin De Becker's great book; Just Two Seconds.

Celebrities have a greater need for protection in the United States than do most Executives, due to their high exposure to the public and the fact that their popularity is generated by a very large population. You read about celebrities all the time. You see them on television, hear them on the radio and watch them in movies. Not so with most Executives. The greatest threat the Celebrity encounters is the enthusiastic fan, the stalker and the paparazzi. Rarely do we hear about a celebrities being kidnapped or attacked in the United States. Celebrity Protection Agents rarely use any type of force in the line-of-duty.

There is much hype and mystery that seems to surround this world of Executive Protection. Here are some quick facts.

- Most graduates of Executive Protection schools never end up securing a job in the Executive Protection field, because there are so few legitimate jobs available.
- Those who do find a legitimate job are quickly educated on the reality of long hours, a meager hourly rate and the realization that much of the work is more akin to that of an administrative assistant than a protection Agent.
- There are approximately 700,000 sworn law enforcement officers in the United States. There are approximately 1 million contract security officers in the United States. There are approximately 1 million guards working directly for United States corporations. Add in some bodyguards and administrative people and you have a total of approximately 3 million people working under the banner of "protective service occupations" in the United States.

- The median salary for people in these occupations is $39,000 annually.
- There are approximately 2.2 million active duty and reserve people in the US Military.
- According to the US Bureau of Labor Statistics, employment of security guards is expected to grow about 14% by 2018. That represents about 152,000 new positions. Demand for guards also will grow as private security firms increasingly perform duties—such as providing security at public events and in residential neighborhoods—that were formerly handled by police officers. Additionally, private security firms are expected to provide more protection to facilities, such as hospitals and nursing homes.
- The few legitimate Executive Protection positions that are available are primarily filled by off duty law enforcement, retired law enforcement and secret service or retired military people with specialized expertise.
- The required training for a private security guard, private detective or protective Agent is non-existent in some states and woefully inadequate and ineffective in most other states.
- The average civilian who lives in a state that allows the possession of a firearm has more statutory authority to defend themselves or others than most people employed in "protective service occupations", primarily due to company policies regarding use of force.
- The median salary for a security guard in the US is $29,000. That is approximately $13.00 an hour.

Next, consider most sources that forecast promising careers over the next decade do not include Executive Protection Agent. Does a security position seem promising to you? As a hopeful Executive Protection Agent, considering the information presented here, where is your money best spent? Don't get me wrong. Many people who have a passion for something will overcome enormous odds to reach their dreams and goals, and you should be encouraged to do so. I simply suggest you use some common sense and make prudent decisions about how you get there.

Add to this the time-honored dilemma that it is relatively easy to find and attend training but almost impossible to gain employment in this field without some experience. How do you get experience if no one will hire you because you have no experience?

If you are interested in becoming involved in the Protection or Security Industry, my suggestion for a career path looks something like this:

- Obtain a BA or BS in Criminal Justice or related field; Law, Psychology, Forensic Science or Homeland Security.
- If you enlist in the military, choose Military Police, Law Enforcement, Intelligence or Special Forces.
- Volunteer with a Fire Department, Police Department or Sheriff's Department Reserve. Many departments have civilian police academies. Attend one.
- Obtain a part-time job in private security as a guard while attending school. These are entry level jobs but will be a welcome addition to your resume.
- Take a good self defense course or enroll in a certified martial arts program. Get a certificate upon completion. Employers like certificates.
- Learn handgun safety and handgun self defense. If you live in a carry state, procure your permit to carry.
- Learn to handle weapons beyond a firearm including pepper spray, kubaton & control instruments, impact weapons and handcuffs.
- Go on-line and find organizations like the Anti Terrorism Accreditation Board, which, for a fee, will certify you as a Certified Anti-Terrorism Specialist upon completing their course.
- Read or join bodyguard and Executive Protection forums online. You can learn a lot from reading them.

Having accomplished these things, not only have you enhanced your ability to actually work in the field of Executive Protection, you also have transferable skills should you decide not to.

If these facts do not sway you from plunking down a few thousand dollars for training, or you are thinking about all the money you can make internationally by working for a private security firm, read "Private Military Contractors and US Grand Strategy" by David Isenberg, who is an independent, Washington-D.C. based analyst and writer on military, foreign policy, national and international security issues and the author of Shadow Force: Private Security Contractors in Iraq. Good luck with that overseas thing!

The former private security company, Blackwater, took such a hit over the debacle in Iraq that massive public relations were needed to try and re-establish their credibility; even to the point of changing the name of the company to Xe. Currently, they are calling themselves Academi. Can you see by the name change how this company is branding and marketing itself? Private security contractors overseas are, at a minimum, controversial.

Additionally, traveling and working abroad carries another risk. Kidnap, Ransom and Extortion is abundant. The average amount paid for reported kidnap cases in 2005 was $62,000. The many unreported cases generate ransoms around several hundred to several thousand dollars. 48% of Kidnap for Ransom incidents occur in Latin America. According to insurance carrier AIG's Crisis Management Division in Philadelphia, "there are over 20,000 reported kidnap for ransom incidents annually, with 48 percent of them occurring in Latin America." 80% of kidnap for ransom cases are left unreported. Estimates are hard to come by, because sources vary wildly in their reporting methods and definitions. The annual incidence of reported and unreported kidnap for ransom cases are probably between 15,000 and 100,000 per year. Most of these kidnap victims are locals, not foreigners.

According to the US State Department, data shows that there are on average 20 to 25 hostage incidents involving Americans overseas each year, and an administration official said that few of them were politically motivated. Most involved requests for ransom.

We live in a global economy in which international travel is frequent and regular for many company employees. Unfortunately, these employees or their families can be targeted for kidnapping based on the perception of wealth that is available for ransom from the company or the family of the employee.

If you are interested in providing protection to people, you may want to explore the arena of kidnapping overseas. It appears by the numbers alone, there is professional employment opportunity here. The US State Department, the FBI and insurance companies like AIG who provide kidnap insurance are good sources to study the topic more closely. Kidnap and Hostage incidents abroad are a problem, but since most of the victims are locals, not foreigners, if this were to become your specialty you would likely have to move overseas.

**Conclusion**

There are a great many "Executive Protection" courses that are traditionally about a week long, held by legitimate instructors, and charging several thousand dollars for the experience. The skills taught at these courses focus on protecting an individual. The transference of these skills into paid employment in the Executive Protection field is difficult at best. If you do attend fee based training, consider courses similar to the Force Science Certification Course sponsored by The Force Science Institute or the Advanced Threat Assessment & Management Academy sponsored by Gavin De Becker & Associates. There is an essential need for critical thinking in the field of Executive Protection which goes far beyond control tactics, martial arts, firearms and positional drills in the field.

There is a lot that the prospective Executive Protection Agent can do that will give them transferable skills for a paid position in private security, the criminal justice system or a related profession.

Finally, if you do pursue a position in the Executive Protection field, it's all about networking. There are a lot of "mom and pop" security companies across the United States. There are good one and bad ones. There are professionals and there are hacks. They all have different niches. One may specialize in "high-end" hotels and bars, another in celebrity protection, or another in insurance fraud. The larger security companies tend to focus on providing uniform guards and plainclothes security services. There are other companies who specialize in event security.

If you want to find an employment position protecting a person, you will need to network heavily with others in the field. One other thing to consider; in many regional areas the "security and protection" community is small. Translation: If you develop a reputation that is less than excellent, a lot of people are going to hear about it very quickly.

**The Bottom Line**
Invest in a long term strategy and spend your money wisely.

# 2
# INTRODUCTION TO THE PRINCIPLES OF PROTECTION

Your mission as an Executive Protection Agent is to insure that the identified Assets you are assigned to protect are not degraded, destroyed or compromised.

This book is an overview of issues that should be evaluated, which serve to neutralize and reduce risk. Keep in mind that this is a guide. The principles are important and may be adapted to a variety of settings which include the Executive in passive or active circumstances; and with a single-man, small or large Executive Protection team.

In other words, this type of work is principle driven. Sound principles work even if you do not get them technically perfect. This book was purposely written in that manner. One of my mentors used to tell me to think like a house painter; not Rembrandt. I always understood this to mean that either way the paint goes on. Years later looking back on that comment, I realize he was talking about the broad themes of physical motor skills and specific techniques of self defense and control tactics. Now, I also understand that as an EP Agent I can carry out my responsibilities in such a manner that people look at me with the same appreciation they have for Rembrandt's paintings, because my work reflects excellence and I display uncommon professionalism.

If you have a background in the criminal justice system - law enforcement, corrections or other public safety assignments - you may find some of these principles challenging your paradigms and beliefs. Public Safety officials make solid attempts to educate the public regarding risk and they often engage in extensive training to prepare for known risks. However, a big part of their *mission* is to respond to, confront and manage emergency situations. They are primarily reacting to a threat rather than proactively observing and mitigating possible risks. Generally, they are trained to *go to the problem*.

Executive Protection is an art form which requires effective, efficient and proactive mitigation and elimination of risk. The Executive Protection professional concentrates on observation and detection of potential risk, with a focus on preventing those risks from becoming an obstacle to their mission. This is in contrast to public safety officials who react to risks and problems as they are reported to them but do not necessarily react to every potential problem out there.

In the event that something presents an imminent threat to the identified Assets, the majority of Executive Protection Agents on a detail should act swiftly to protect and remove the Asset from the threat. Fewer resources (agents) will actually move to confront the problem. Again, this is in stark contrast to the public safety or criminal justice professional, where most of the resources go to confront the problem.

Simply put, public safety professionals go to the problem. EP Agents remove the Asset from the problem. The mission focus and use of resources are different.

Additionally, public safety or criminal justice professionals have statutory and perceived authority which lends a sense of power to any of their actions. The EP Agent has no such authority. The Executive Protection Agent's duties may include diverting an assailant, driving the Executive to an appointment, waiting for hours in a hotel room or running the Executive's personal errands. The EP Agent must be prepared to eliminate threat with split-second decision making, yet be appropriate in high-powered social settings while multi-tasking. These typically basic responsibilities of the EP Agent are very different than that of the public safety or criminal justice professional.

Because of these diverse responsibilities, I refer to the function of the Executive Protection as Ballet. Think of it as Ballet on steroids. Ballet is defined as: "A classical dance form characterized by grace and precision of movement and by elaborate formal gestures, steps, and poses." Take the word, "dance", out of this definition and you have a Zen-type definition of the Executive Protection function.

## General Principles of Protection

Your responsibilities as an EP Agent include insuring that the identified Asset/s are not degraded, destroyed or compromised. You and your team will accomplish this through observation and detection of risk. You will then take any necessary action to reduce and neutralize risk.

There are different degrees of risk. The Executive Protection professional must determine the level of risk in any given situation and environment. Then, they must determine what level of risk is acceptable.

## Evaluating Risk

In general, when considering risk to the Principal (also known as the Executive or the Asset), you should be asking some of the following questions.

- What is the probability of injury, damage or loss? What reasonable security measures can be taken to neutralize the probability of injury, damage and loss?
- Does the physical location have inherent risk like sharp corners, active movement, stairs, hidden hallways or rooms? Can the physical location be changed to another location where sharp corners, active movement, stairs, hidden hallways or rooms are not part of the environment?
- Are there obvious circumstances that raise the degree of risk? For instance, is the Principal meeting in a war-torn part of the world where terrorism is active? Can the meeting take place in a more secure setting?
- Are you protecting someone who has known threats against them? Have known threats been investigated?
- What appropriate procedures may be implemented to neutralize potential, demonstrated or specific probable risks? Example: The direction and flow of people is the key to managing public events. If there are 15 public entrances to a venue can those be reduced to a few entrances so Agents can screen and observe the behavioral characteristics of people attending?
- Can adjoining rooms be swept and secured ahead of time?
- Can a route be screened prior to travel?

An acceptable risk policy is required because for every potential risk you discover, you will need to make a decision as to how you will address that risk. How you evaluate risk ultimately determines whether you will address them with resources.

When assessing risk you should assign High, Medium and Low risk values. These definitions will be shared later in the book, but by actually assigning a value you will be able to quickly decide whether you should dedicate resources to the risk or not. What risks are acceptable? Example: If a parking area is assigned a Low risk value, does it require a "posted" Agent position?

You may have to accept certain levels of risk depending on the chain of command and the structure of authority you are working under. Your decisions regarding risk may be over-ridden by the Principal, local authorities or the people who hired you.

What follows are a number of other issues that should be taken into consideration. At first glance this can be mind-boggling, but it will become second-nature as you continue to study and work in the world of Executive Protection.

Hostile Behavior and Personal Attacks
- Has anyone specifically been identified that may present this type of behavior?
- Has any "class" of individuals been identified as potential or likely Adversaries?
- If hostile behavior erupts, how will it be communicated to the people responsible to deal with it and how will it be handled?

Note: Recognizing, knowing and understanding the likely Adversary, Methods of the Adversary and likely Targets will give the Executive Safety Professional an advantage in strategic planning and tactics. This is a critical part of Risk Assessment and is presented later in the book. Example: If the likely Adversary is a Terrorist, counter-terrorist tactics should be considered which are significantly different than those tactics employed against the rogue individual with Mental Health issues and instability.

Threats From Inside and Outside
How will they be detected, reported and handled?

Accidental and Environmental Problems
Are there significant accidental and environmental concerns? Examples: Sharp objects, loose steps; an insecticide company spraying nearby.

Political
What general and specific political realities need to be taken into consideration? Example: Is the Principal speaking about the virtues of eating beef in a heavily populated Hindu area?

Places
Some places are inherently more risky than others. Example: A structure made of ICF construction will withstand a strong earthquake, while a stick-built building is not nearly as bullet-proof or explosion resistant.

- Is there a great amount of glass exposure? The greatest injuries incurred from a blast or explosion is from glass.
- Is the neighborhood known to have high criminal activity?

## Basic Common Security Components
All of these components must be considered. The Principal is the person you are protecting. The Asset is the thing you are protecting. These terms are interchangeable. Who are the people or Assets you are *required* to protect? Do not confuse your Mission! If you are assigned to protect an Asset you should not be distracted by other things.

The Staff
- Who is with the Principal or accompanying the identified Asset? Often, there is a primary person who works for the Principal as some type of administrative assistant. These people are invaluable when determining schedules and the personal preferences of the Principal.
- What other staff will be accompanying the Principal?

The Tenants
- Who works in the area?
- Are there regularly assigned staff in the building or the location you will be at? Do not confuse staff with the general public.
- If there are staff members in the area, have they been screened?
- Is staff clearly identified? Note: "Insiders" are often used in assassination attempts.

Extra Staff
There may be adjunct or auxiliary Security available to support the Mission. If available, they should be identified and integrated into the function.

The Press
The Press can be a hindrance or be helpful. With public figures, the Press may often be present. Some Press members may become an unintended diversion by violating the personal space of the Principal or by their use of cameras. The Press should be dealt with fairly and firmly. The wise Principal will take a moment to allow for pictures which will often satisfy the Press and resolve any unintended diversions from them. Otherwise, inserting Security

Personnel between the Principal and the Press is generally an acceptable option.

## The General Public
- The direction and flow of people is the key to managing any event.
- Where will the Public arrive?
- How will the Public be "routed"?
- Will there be any screening of the Public?
- Will the Public be identified in any manner?

## Deliveries
How will any deliveries be handled and screened?

## Packages & Mail
How will any packages be handled and screened?

## All Areas & Rooms
Have areas been screened through great Site Advance work? Areas have the potential to hide things. Therefore, look for areas in which things can be hidden. Example: False ceilings are a great place to hide things, as are cupboards. Most people, including protection Agents, don't look up when they are walking. They look down or straight ahead. As an Executive Safety professional you cannot afford to miss anything. Make it a habit to scan the complete horizon and to look for hidden objects within an area, or objects on top of cupboards and shelves. Don't forget to check the ceiling.

NOTE: The Adversary will try to divert your attention. The Adversary may know how you think. Adversaries need to get reasonably close to attack. Most attacks occur at arrival and departure areas. Therefore, plan significantly for these things.

## The Protective Detail Mission
In a general sense, your primary responsibility when you are protecting an Asset is the following. I use the acronym DIG, because it makes sense. You are constantly "digging" to discover threats. The very notion of digging requires that you investigate beyond what you see on the surface.

**DIG:** Discover, Investigate, Guard = DIG.

*Discover* risks and potential problems from as many angles and as far away as possible. This makes post placement critical. A post placement is where you would position yourself or another EP Agent to provide protection. In order to Discover you need to be able to be in a position to do so. Look for unusual and inappropriate behavior. Once discovered, some type of evaluation and/or investigation should take place. Discover defined is: To notice or learn, especially by making an effort; To be the first, or the first of one's group or kind, to find, learn of, or observe; To learn about for the first time in one's experience; To learn something about; To identify a person as a potential problem or Adversary; To reveal or expose.

*Investigate* inappropriate or unusual people, behavior or things you have discovered. Investigate identified risks and potential problems. This can be accomplished using various methods. An Agent or ancillary security may have direct contact with the inappropriate or unusual person, behavior or thing you have discovered. The Principle may be re-routed. The inappropriate or unusual person or behavior may be re-routed. Investigate defined is: To inquire into a situation or problem thoroughly in order to discover the truth.

*Guard* the Principle from risks and problems. There are a number of methods and techniques that can be used to guard your Asset. It depends on the Asset and the scope of the problem. Guard defined is: To protect from harm by or as if by watching over; To watch over so as to prevent escape or violence; To keep (an opposing player) from scoring or playing efficiently; To maintain control over, as to prevent indiscretion; To supervise entry or exit through; keep watch at; To escort.

The greatest danger closest to the Principal needs immediate attention. Danger farther away from the Principal Asset needs evaluation, but you have more time to react. Be prepared to react to less than clear aggression. People's behavior is not always telegraphed. Not all aggression is immediately apparent. Remember aggression usually involves physical movement.

If violence suddenly does erupt or there is an actual emergency that presents imminent threat to the well-being of the Principal, you will kick things into an emergency response mode. I use the acronym SAV for the Executive Protection Agent's emergency response because it makes as much sense as DIG does. The very notion of "saving" someone requires that you get them out of harm's way. The Agent's emergency response should look like this.

**SAV:** Shelter, Alarm, Vacate = SAV.

*Shelter* the Asset/Principal. This, by definition, requires that more Agents go to the Principal to shelter or evacuate them. Fewer Agents go to the problem and preferably the Agent closest to the problem deals with it. Shelter defined is: Something that provides cover or protection; a refuge; a haven; the state of being covered or protected.

Sound the *Alarm*. Alarm defined is: A warning of existing or approaching danger; an electrical, electronic, or mechanical device that serves to warn of danger by means of a sound or signal; a call to arms. It is entirely possible that you may be dealing with sudden violence or an emergency in one place, while Agents at other post positions are completely unaware of what is happening. This depends on the size and scope of your protection mission and detail. Other Agents need to be notified through reliable and accurate communication what is happening if an emergency erupts.

*Vacate* the area. You have two choices in an emergency. You should remove the Principal. If your Asset is an object, and it is a fixed thing you cannot easily move – you may have to neutralize the threat by confronting it directly rather than moving the Asset. Vacate defined is: To cease to occupy or hold; give up; to empty of occupants or incumbents.

## The Attack

When you really think about it there are only so many types of people and only so many methods of attacking someone. If we remove dangerous objects that fly though the air - like bullets, rocks, grenades, missiles or thrown blunt objects – protecting a Principal is not that difficult *if* the Principal will let you do your job effectively. That means you maintain two arm's-length distance between a potential Adversary and the Principal. At this distance, there are no attacks that can be delivered by an Adversary's hands or feet. The greater the distance between the Adversary and your Principal, the less likely the Adversary can position themselves properly to attack your Principal using their hands or feet. The greater the distance, the safer everyone will be.

Conversely, and seemingly contradictive, the closer you are to an Adversary who would attempt an attack on your Principal, the greater your ability to successfully intervene. Under circumstances in which the Principal must have close contact with people, the EP Agent must be positioned in a manner that allows them to react quickly to a threat. This means that EP Agents must be positioned within two arm's-length of the potential Adversary or the Principal. Why? To either quickly move the Principal or engage the Adversary with successful intervention.

Action is quicker than reaction. Once an Adversary initiates an attack, it takes your brain a few precious fractions of a second to assess that which is beginning to unfold – and then come up with an appropriate response to it. According to Gavin De Becker's research of public attacks that are detailed in his book; Just Two Seconds, most public attacks are over within 5 seconds. A lot can happen in 5 seconds and your brain can actually process a lot of information in that time. As an EP Agent you want every advantage you can get and distance is your primary tool. Distance creates time. Time for you to DIG and extra time to SAV if need be. For instance, if an attack begins and you are 12 feet away versus 3 feet away your ability to successfully intervene drops dramatically.

The bottom line is that an Adversary needs to get close enough to attack the Principal. Don't let it happen. And in those circumstances that the two arm-length rule cannot be maintained between the public and the Principal, then an EP Agent must maintain it by virtue of their positioning - between themselves, the public and the Principal.

What about those things that fly through the air; bullets, rocks, grenades, missiles or thrown blunt objects? Well, it helps to understand the nature of these attacks, because if we know how most attacks are delivered, we also know how to prepare for most attacks.

Citing more statistics from De Becker's Just 2 Seconds:
- Lone Adversaries account for 87% of attacks in the United States.
- Outside the United States this figure is almost inverted. 71% of attacks have multiple Adversaries outside the US.
- Attacks in the US are almost evenly divided between indoors and outdoors.
- 71% of these attacks come using some type of firearms; with handguns being used 51% of the time and long guns (rifles) being used 20%. The reverse is true outside the US, where long guns are used more often.
- Most attacks in the US are at less than 25 feet. This is true outside the US as well even though long guns are used more often. Creating space buffers of more than 25 feet almost guarantees the Principal's safety.
- Better and more available Emergency Medical Services in the US reduces the death and injury rate of attacks.
- Bombs are about as successful as often as they fail. They fail 57% of the time.

- 64% of attacks occur around the Principal's vehicle and 77% of those attacks are successful. Therefore, be critically aware of arrivals and departures.

Distance facts: Many successful attacks could have been avoided by screening and limiting access to the area that the attack was staged; to authorized people only.

- When an attack begins and the EP Agent is 15 feet from the Adversary, the Adversary is likely to prevail.
- At 7 feet it is a very close contest.
- If the EP Agent is within arms-reach there is no contest at all. The EP Agent wins.
- With one EP Agent in the proper position covering the Principle and another Agent is on the Adversary, EP Agents will prevail almost every time.
- If the Agent is more than 25 feet from the Principal when the attack begins, the Agent will have NO impact on the outcome.

Weapons facts:
- 49% of attacks occur with handguns.
- 29% of attacks occur with long rifles, or rifles.
- Explosive devices are used in 15% of attacks, but 70% of those are delivered through the mail, so the EP Agent will probably have little influence on the outcome. This is a procedural mail delivery and screening issue for the Principal.
- 5% of attacks occur with knives and edged weapons.
- 2% are fists.

Given this impressive set of facts, you can see that a lot of your success is going to be predicated on the degree to which your Principal will allow you to operate within the space you need to protect them from these statistics. I am fully aware that some VIP's do not want someone in their space-bubble. It can feel intrusive to them. Part of your effectiveness as an EP Agent is to have a discussion with the Principal in which these facts are appropriately discussed.

**General Positioning**
Keeping these facts in the forefront of your mind will almost guarantee success in an Executive Protection detail. Here are some other specific things you can do to further alter the odds in your favor.

- React to gross motor movement near the Principle. Gross motor movements are generally large muscle movement of the arms and legs. Most attacks are delivered by an Adversary's arms (hands) and legs. The sudden movement of arms, hands and legs near the Principal needs to be evaluated rapidly.
- Talk with your hands above your waist. This allows them to react more quickly to violence if it suddenly erupts, as opposed to having them by your side (action vs. reaction).
- Play TAG. Much like the game you played as a child, TAG puts distance between you (or the Principal) and an Adversary. TAG allows you to manage the attack. As long as you are two arm's-length away from an Adversary they cannot touch you, hit you, grab you, punch you, stab you or kick you.
- Bullets and objects thrown fly through the air. In these instances you would want to be close enough to divert the firearm, take the firearm away or take the weapon away from the Adversary. To accomplish this successfully, given the statistics cited, you must be within two arm's-length distance of the threat. There are several ways to quickly interfere with a physical attack. In the case of a physical assault with hands, you need to get your hands moving like two windshield wipers to ward off and block the attack.
- Control the Adversary's hands inside of their clothing if you believe there to be potential danger because their hands are in their pockets.
- Familiarize yourself with simple control techniques for moving people, disarming weapons and knives, and weaponless control techniques.
- Move from the center. Turn or go away from danger with the Principal.
- Divide the response between the Principal and the threat. The majority of Agents should move toward the Principal.
- In the event of an unspecified threat, shrink the perimeters.

## Taking It To The Next Level

Many, if not most, Police Departments, Sheriff's Departments, Fire Departments, Department of Natural Resources, Game & Fish, The Forest Service and other public service agencies or law enforcement agencies have something called a "Ride Along" program, whether it be formal or informal. Contact one of these agencies and speak to them about riding along with and observing one of their employees. The point of this practical exercise is to observe the mission of these professionals. Look for the differences between reactive and proactive behavior. The proactive behavior you observe is more aligned with the mission of the Executive Protection Agent.

# 3
# TEAMWORK

Lt. Colonel Dave Grossman, author of <u>On Combat</u>, writes: "If you have no capacity for violence then you are a healthy productive citizen, a sheep. If you have a capacity for violence and no empathy for your fellow citizens, then you have defined an aggressive sociopath, a wolf. But what if you have a capacity for violence, and a deep love for your fellow citizens? What do you have then? A sheepdog, a warrior, someone who is walking the hero's path. Someone who can walk into the heart of darkness, into the universal human phobia, and walk out unscathed."

The Sheepdog is the person who naturally walks towards trouble instead of running from it. Working amongst these warriors is a lot of fun and a privilege. These are my people. They are the ones that are attracted to positions within the Military Services, the Criminal Justice System, Private Security, Fire Departments and Emergency Medical Services.

One of the most powerful principles of managing violent behavior is this; when two or more people are present, risk is reduced by up to 80%. When three or more are present, the risk of violence is reduced up to 95%. Also, the more EP Agents you have on a protection detail, the greater the ability to DIG. It's that simple. The more, the merrier.

However, with any group of Agents there are several unknown wildcards; their actual ability as measured by their training and talent, and their ability to work well with others. I have worked with some exceptional people and on some great teams. I have also watched as one Agent screwed things up beyond comprehension through their ignorance and arrogance.

## Self

I have spent over 35 years working in the criminal justice system, private security, fugitive apprehension, executive protection, probation & parole, correctional facilities and asset protection. I have served on SWAT teams and was an investigator with a bomb squad. I was an arson investigator. I have taught, lectured and written articles on a variety of subjects regarding use of force and safety. I have been mentored by some of the most brilliant minds in these areas. I have had incredible opportunities to travel in the course of these activities. I am an avid researcher and am fascinated with human behavior. I have been around a lot of violence and understand the dynamics of this animal well. I share this for *one* reason. In all these experiences I have observed one thing that above all else, stands in the way of excellence. It is *self*.

Many people who are inherently drawn to this type of work are proud, macho, self-reliant, independent, and sometimes arrogant. The actual work performed tends to reinforce those qualities. Indeed, strong personalities are essential for success in protection work but they need to be brought under the influence of something greater than the single Agent. Properly harnessed by Excellence, these rogue personalities will begin to absorb the characteristics associated with confidence, courage, teamwork, understanding, humility, servitude and power – true warriors.

There will always be differences among us. We are all unique with our own special characteristics. But the need for denial of self will become apparent in this type of work.

Conversely, a certain degree of respectful disagreement can be helpful. Exploring diverse ideas and viewpoints in a respectful manner will most often bring about the best result, solution or plan. The denial of self cannot be so exaggerated that you are ineffective. If you feel strongly about something, speak up. If you see potential risk, it needs to be acted on. If, during advance work you notice something has been overlooked, it should be exposed.

It is not within these expressions that *self* becomes an obstacle. It is within the internal dynamics of the heart's motivation that *self* becomes an obstacle. For instance, someone who expresses a view or opinion may feel slighted because their view was rejected. What happens next? Does anger, pride or resentment begin to stir in that heart? Perhaps that heart carries a fear of rejection going all the way back to childhood and the perception that their view is being ignored is pushing all those buttons; "No one cares about what I think!" It is the manner in which *self* is expressed and that internal reaction when *self* feels slighted that becomes a stumbling block.

23

We all express ourselves in different ways. The choice of words and tone of voice can be interpreted and misinterpreted many different ways. For instance, people have been telling me for years that my delivery of a viewpoint can be very direct, often blunt and might be taken offensively by others. I don't purposely plan to offend people. Yet, I understand this personality characteristic of mine and have taken the time to figure out how to best deal with it. My personality type is one that naturally gravitates away from small talk and wants to get to the root of the matter as quickly as possible. That's how I am wired. Because I understand this, I try to take the time to tell people that my delivery might be uncommonly direct and that I mean no offense by it. I do not naturally possess the gracious social skills that a terrific sales person might have. I am not a fan of spending a great deal of effort in correcting weaknesses. I recognize my weaknesses, but prefer to focus on my unique strengths and what they can add to the team. That is where I will be most effective. But I need to recognize this in order to be able to communicate effectively with others.

On another note, although Teamwork is essential to Executive Protection success, democracies do not work well in this profession and particularly during an Executive Protection function. Someone needs to be in charge. Roles needs to be defined. The work environment needs to be respectful, open, honest and creative. Why creative? The best EP Agents I know can make quick decisions and adjust as needed in a variety of settings. This requires creativity.

**What is Teamwork?**
Teamwork is defined in the Business Dictionary as: "The process of working collaboratively with a group of people, in order to achieve a goal. Teamwork is often a crucial part of a business, as it is often necessary for colleagues to work well together, trying their best in any circumstance. Teamwork means that people will try to cooperate, using their individual skills and providing constructive feedback, despite any personal conflict between individuals."

**Why Should We Be Interested in Teamwork?**
The short answer to this is because without it, you will raise the risk of violence and the risk of failure to your mission - which is to protect something or someone.

I have had the privilege of working with some organizations for long periods of time - up to a year – consulting, assisting and teaching them about executive protection and asset protection. From those experiences I share the most significant lessons I know about developing effective teams. The core concepts, which I have elaborated on, come from Larson and LaFasto in their book titled <u>Teamwork: What Must Go Right/What Can Go Wrong</u>.

Teams need to have clear goals. This is why you complete, to the best of your ability, the Planning Checklist presented later in the book. By completing it you will have effectively defined the goal and communicated it precisely.

Teams should have a results-driven structure. Democracies do not work well in this profession. Benevolent dictators are better. Having acknowledged that you need to give your team leaders and Agents enough discretion to make decisions on their own. Additionally, it would be in the team's best interest to determine who is good at what. If one of your Agents is a former sniper, why would you post that Agent on the jump team? If one of your Agents is a skilled martial artist with practical experience around violence, why would you post that Agent on the outer perimeter? Determine your team's strengths and weaknesses and use them to your advantage.

The team must have competent team members. Refer to the previous comments. Determine your team member's strengths and weaknesses and assign them to posts that can utilize those skill sets.

The team must have unified commitment. As I mentioned, there are a fair share of people who get into this profession for the wrong reasons. I understand you may not have the ability to hire or terminate the people you work with. I also understand that you may not be able to give every potential Agent you work with a psychological evaluation – although they should all probably have one. And, you probably do not have the time or the inclination to determine the deep psychological reasons someone would even want to do this type of work. Professionalism is the key word here. Protection Agents that do not display professionalism will not be committed to a unified goal.

The team must have a collaborative climate. It is a climate of trust produced by honest, open, consistent and respectful behavior. With this climate teams perform well. Without it, they fail. You cannot teach trust. Trust is built through relationships. It is built between team members as they get to know each other and work together. One of the quickest methods of building trust is to train together, and on a regular basis.

The team must have high standards that are understood by all. Team members must know what is expected of them individually and collectively. This is, at its core, all about professionalism. Excellence should never be sacrificed and the lack of it should not be tolerated. If you are a leader, make sure your communications are clear. Ask Agents to repeat back to you things

25

that are critical. Perception is everything, and different people will interpret words and statements differently. One of the most often-heard statements that come in a debriefing after a mistake on a detail is this: "I thought you meant......"

The team must receive external support and encouragement. This is not rocket science. Good work deserves praise and bad work requires accountability.

The team must have principled leadership. Pick your leaders wisely.

There are many assignments in the field of Executive Protection in which you will find yourself working alone or with a small detail. In these instances, proactive planning and site advance field work may not even be possible. However, the principles of teamwork will still be applicable because, in a single-agent assignment or in a small detail you will be required to communicate and coordinate activities from time to time with other entities and officials.

If you are involved in the planning of a large event or detail, it is advisable to have a senior team assembled in order to delegate specific tasks. Efficient teamwork is a critical factor in the successful planning of any detail, and in carrying out the responsibilities associated with Executive Protection.

## Taking It To The Next Level
First, get on a computer and find Lt. Colonel Dave Grossman's article; On Sheep, Wolves and Sheepdogs. Read it.

Next, write a paragraph or two regarding how these principles apply to your life, from a personal, emotional and/or spiritual perspective. There is no right or wrong for this essay.

It should cause you to think about your potential effectiveness as an EP Agent. If you are wired as a Sheepdog and are a true team player, you are well on your way to being successful amongst those who protect Assets as part of their vocation.

# 4
# THE LEGAL ISSUES

It is absolutely imperative that you understand how the legal aspects of self defense affect your ability to protect an Asset. This is why I strongly recommend that you take a self defense course or enroll in a martial arts discipline that teaches the legal aspects of self defense as part of their curriculum.

There should be three key questions that EP Agents ask when considering how they are going to physically protect their Asset.
- What is Legal?
- What is the Mission?
- What does statute or policy allow or restrict?

This book does not cover Use of Force, except to the degree presented in this chapter. Suffice it to say that in the United States, in every state, there is a general legal ability to physically intervene in a situation which presents the risk of injury, great bodily harm or death to yourself or another.

If you have an interest in Executive Protection you should find a good self defense course and complete it. You do not need to be a black-belt martial artist or a nationally ranked competitive firearms expert to participate in this profession. You do, however, need to have some basic motor skill ability that focuses on controlling people's movements. I offer several courses to groups that are available through my website at AssaultPrevention.Org. These courses are heavily undergirded in the legal aspects of using force. Although I am a firm believer in the courses and curriculums I have created, I recommend that you try and find a local course first and take it in-person. Participating in-person has great value.

## Use of Force

For travel within the United States, Use of Force is governed by state law; that being the laws of the state you find yourself in. It is a good idea to research those statutes before working in that state.

Executive Protection professionals have no greater statutory authority that that granted to a civilian in any given state, so when I watch video of Brad Pitt's bodyguard grabbing paparazzi by the throat and slamming them up into a wall while "having the chat" with them – I know I am watching an assault. Unless this bodyguard can articulate that his perception was that this paparazzi was about to do something that would cause injury to someone; we call it an assault. There are ways to move people out of the way without assaulting them.

Most states will allow the reasonable Use of Force to prevent harm to yourself or others, or theft of property. Control instruments, impact weapons, stun guns, flashlights and pepper sprays are not banned from airline check-through baggage, and these items are also legal for civilians to carry in most states. These are great tools for the EP Agent to carry - legally. Check ahead as to the statutory restrictions on these items before you enter any state. If you are flying and anticipate taking these items with you, call the airline first to determine what their policies are for each item.

Generally, in the United States, the right of self-defense allows a person attacked to use reasonable force in their own defense and the defense of others. While the statutes defining the legitimate use of force in defense of a person vary from state to state, the general rule makes an important distinction between the use of physical force and *deadly* physical force.

A person may use physical force to prevent imminent physical injury; however a person may not use deadly physical force unless that person is in reasonable fear of serious physical injury or death.

Many statutes also include a duty to retreat, wherein deadly physical force may only be used if the person acting in self defense is unable to safely retreat. A person is generally not obligated to retreat if in one's own home (for example, a person doesn't have to retreat from the living room to the kitchen, then to the bedroom, then to the bathroom) in what has come to be called the "castle exception" (derived from the expression, "A man's home is his castle"). These are also referred to as "stand your ground" laws.

The Castle Doctrine, in essence, simply places into law what is a fundamental right; self-defense. If a person is in a place he or she has a right to be—in the front yard, on the road, working in their office, strolling through the park—and is confronted by an armed predator, he or she can respond with force in defense of their lives. The Castle Doctrine also protects the law-abiding citizen from criminal and civil charges for defending themselves against an attacker whereby, after enduring the trauma of a violent attack they are not dragged through some weird, nightmarish legal battle that could derail their financial future.

Another wildcard: Not every state has passed Castle Doctrine laws, which means that in some states you may have to consider retreating, but even in most of those states the law talks about "reasonable" retreat. A reasonable retreat would not be leaving your Principal (presumably the person paying you to protect them) alone and exposed to a threat while you slink out the back door. If you are protecting a VIP the law does not expect you to abandon them and retreat if possible, because your mission is to protect them.

For the most part, you can use "reasonable" force if needed to intervene in circumstances in which you believe yourself or someone else in going to suffer injury, harm or death. This begs the question: What is "reasonable"? Since EP Agents have generally the same powers and authority as civilians, read on. It will put much of this into perspective.

### Civilian Use of Force in Self-defense: What Are the Standards?

Consider this. You've just finished buying groceries one evening and are on the way to your vehicle when you are confronted by a stranger who demands your money. You push him away in an attempt to escape. He trips and falls, hitting his head against the ground. The police arrive and everything is sorted out. You are sent on your way and the stranger is carted off to the hospital. You find out several days later that the stranger died due to the traumatic brain injury he received when his head hit the ground. Several weeks later, you are served papers which indicate you are being sued by the stranger's family for wrongful death due to your negligence. Is this possible?

The central idea behind a wrongful death lawsuit is that through negligence, carelessness or recklessness, someone died. These lawsuits, usually brought forth on behalf of the surviving family members, attempt to collect damages for expenses related to the death, pain and suffering experienced by the survivors and for future earnings of the deceased.

There is also the possibility of a personal injury lawsuit in which the injured party attempts to collect damages for their injuries based on negligence or intentional wrongdoing.

What rights do civilians have when using force to prevent injury to themselves or others? What are the legal limitations and implications on use of force by civilians? What legal thresholds will be examined by the courts? What specific type of force can be used in self-defense?

To answer these questions, let's look at this from another perspective.

## The Odds of Death

Consider the following odds of death as they relate to personal risk. These numbers vary to some degree depending on the annual totals. These odds are calculated by the National Safety Council on the most recently released data from 2004.

Plane Crash
- One per year odds are 1 in 400,000.
- Lifetime odds are 1 in 5,000.
- In this context, would the Court consider it unusual or negligent for flight attendants to skip the safety instructions given to passengers?

Accidental Drowning
- One per year odds are 1 in 88,772.
- Lifetime odds are 1 in 1,140.
- In this context, would the Court consider it unusual or negligent for the owner of a pool to ignore reasonable efforts towards adult supervision while inviting young neighborhood children to use the pool anytime they wish?

Falls
- One per year odds are 1 in 15,614.
- Lifetime odds are 1 in 200.
- In this context, would the Court consider it unusual or negligent for the owner of a home to invite others over for a barbeque on the upper deck, knowing the guard rails are loose and broken?

Accidental poisoning
- One-year odds are 1 in 14,107.
- Lifetime odds are 1 in 180.

- In this context, would the Court consider it unusual or negligent for the owner of a business to have unidentified hazardous materials in the break room?

Motor Vehicle Accident
- One-year odds are 1 in 6,535.
- Lifetime odds are 1 in 84.
- In this context, would the Court consider it unusual or negligent for automobile manufacturers to sell automobiles without safety restraints?

Utilizing the same formula, I've calculated the following odds regarding crime:

Assault
- One-year odds are 1 in 25,263.
- Lifetime odds are 1 in 217.
- In this context, would the Court consider it unusual or negligent for the intended victim to use force to escape or protect themselves?

The odds of being a victim of any type of crime are approximately 8%. In this context, would the Court consider it unusual or negligent for the intended victim to use force to escape or protect themselves?

The odds of being a victim of violent crime, not necessarily involving death, are 1-2%. In this context, would the Court consider it unusual or negligent for the intended victim to use force to escape or protect themselves?

**What Does The Law Allow?**
Almost all states within the United States allow civilians to use reasonable force in protection of their own or someone else's property or life. Check your own state statutes, as they vary considerably from state to state.

Most of these statutes do not define what reasonable force is. Using the example we began with, is it reasonable to push someone down who is demanding your money, but is not displaying a weapon or threatening you with a weapon? This is where it gets problematic. For argument's sake let's assume that the stranger, who died from the brain injury after you pushed him was found to have a concealed knife in his pocket? Does this make any difference?

Let's change the scenario. The same stranger produces a handgun and demands your money. You, being a legally licensed handgun permit holder, pull your handgun and shoot him. He dies. The police discover the handgun he pulled is really a BB gun, or a toy gun. Does this change your liability?

The bottom line is that the courts will look at several factors.

- Do you have the legal, statutory authority to use force, and under what conditions?
- Were those conditions present at the time of the incident?
- Were you a reluctant participant? Did you create or exacerbate the problem?
- Did you consider retreating? Was it reasonable to consider retreating?
- Was the force you used reasonable, given your perception of the events?

The problem most civilians confront when using force is that they do not understand what is reasonable. The legal definition of reasonable is: "What is appropriate for a particular situation?" This definition is generally applied in the law of Negligence. It is the standard of care that a reasonably prudent person would observe under a certain set of conditions. Someone who exercises such standards would not be negligent.

Let's go back to our example. Is it reasonable for the intended victim to push a stranger away who is demanding their money? Of course it is. We frequently hear about death and injuries that result from these types of crimes. If the civilian's perception is that they are about to be hurt or injured as a result of a crime, it is reasonable to use force to escape.

Was it reasonable for the civilian to shoot the stranger demanding money, when the gun the stranger was using is a toy gun? Yes, it is. The civilian has no duty or obligation to ask the stranger if the gun he is holding in his hand is a toy gun or a BB gun. The civilian's perception at the time of the incident is that the stranger is holding a real gun with real bullets, and he might shoot. Civilians do not have the same *mission* as law enforcement officers have. Police are required by their mission and policy to respond to, and deal with, circumstances that may require use of force. Civilians are not required to get involved in any situation requiring the use of force. Civilians are not sent out to intervene in anything. Civilians can walk away from everything.

Civilians do, however, have almost the same *authority* as police officers when it comes to statutory authority governing the use of force. Civilians have the right to use "reasonable force", as do the police, if their perception is that an Adversary is trying to hurt someone.

In most states, deadly force, or the taking of another's life, is justified if a civilian's perceptions of the activity taking place will likely result in great bodily harm or death. This is the same general rule for police officers. The difference is that civilians must consider retreating, and must be a "reluctant participant", which means they have little choice with being caught up in the circumstances to begin with. Law enforcement personnel do not have these restrictions.

Although not the focus of this chapter, another commonality between police and civilians is the ability to use reasonable force to detain someone during an arrest. In many states civilians can make citizen arrests under certain conditions. Check your state statutes for details.

Law enforcement professionals are held to a higher standard of training than civilians, which is why a Use of Force Model of some type is typically part of law enforcement training. The challenge for the civilian is to determine what is reasonable should they decide to use force. Reasonableness and timeliness are the two primary considerations a judge or jury will use to decide if the civilian's actions were acceptable in a use-of-force case. There are direct parallels to any use of force that an Executive Protection Agent might use.

Traditional martial arts and self-defense classes teach motor skills and techniques, however, they do not teach what is reasonable and timely. It's important that the civilian has a legal framework of force to work within.

Here's an example of the dilemma: A civilian comes upon an Adversary who is standing several feet from another person, fists clenched, swearing, and threatening that other person. The Adversary pushes that person hard, knocking them to the ground. Would it be reasonable for the civilian observing this, who has the right to use force, to intervene in the situation and to purposefully break the Adversary's leg? Probably not. Unfortunately, this is a possible response for the civilian participating in traditional martial arts. Why? Many martial arts will teach you a number of techniques to deal with an Adversary, several of which will break an Adversary's leg.

Now, take the same situation and apply what you will learn from an appropriate Use of Force Model. The description above is one of an Adversary whose actions are physically aggressive with no apparent weapons in hand. A good Use of Force Model will recommend appropriate techniques for this specific type of Adversary. Impact pressure would be one of the appropriate techniques, as would a striking technique. Impact pressure can be applied in ways that do not break a leg yet is still very effective on this type of Adversary. Strikes can also be very effective in a situation like this.

A good Use of Force Model does not teach civilians to break legs. It does, however, suggest that impact pressure and striking specific areas of the body are appropriate responses. Let's assume the civilian performs a brachial stun on the Adversary, which momentarily affects the Adversary's nervous system to the point they collapse and/or lose consciousness. See the difference? Momentary loss of consciousness is considered more reasonable than a broken leg in this particular situation.

Let's change this scenario one more time. The civilian uses a thigh stun or knee strike, which is an appropriate technique on this type of Adversary. The civilian aims for the Adversary's thigh with his knee, but the Adversary turns at the last moment toward the civilian, whose thigh stun ends up striking the Adversary's knee, breaking the knee joint.

In this instance, using either the traditional martial arts training or a Use of Force Model, the injury to the Adversary is the same; a broken leg. But the context and framework is entirely different, and that will affect the considerations of timeliness and reasonableness from a legal perspective.

Primary Consideration: Do your homework when choosing self-defense training and defense weapons. Make sure that the techniques you learn are in the context of a Use of Force Model that has been tested by the courts and is appropriate for civilians. These programs are very difficult to find.

**Firearms**
Executive Protection Agents are always encouraged to be armed to the extent it is legal and your employer allows it. I would encourage you to acquire a permit to carry a firearm in the state you live.

Most Executive Protection Agents that work in a private capacity and travel out of state frequently do not carry firearms. The main reason for this is that the statutes regarding firearms can vary greatly from state to state, wherein the Agent might be required to procure multiple permits from a lot of different states. If the Agent travels internationally it gets even more complicated. Of course, many states have reciprocal agreements with other states if you do have a permit in the state you reside. Checking for these reciprocal agreements should be part of your pre-planning before you travel.

An EP assignment may take you across the United States or around the world. If traveling abroad you should research the country, customs and laws of those places you will be working. Any time the Executive Protection Agent travels outside of their home state they should check the statutes regarding use of force and self defense. As a matter of professionalism it is the Agent's due diligence to complete this.

## Taking It To The Next Level

Find and review your state statutes regarding self defense. Simply go to a search engine and type in: "(your state) statutes regarding use of force, self defense, justifiable taking of life". After reviewing them answer the following questions.

- What are the statutes that govern self defense and use of force in your state?
- What are the statutes that govern deadly force, lethal force or justifiable taking of life in your state?
- Give several examples, based on these statutes, of when you might be able to use reasonable force.
- In your position as an EP Agent, do you have a duty to retreat?
- Can you use reasonable force to intervene if someone is trying to hurt you or someone else?
- Can you use reasonable force to intervene if someone is trying to take yours or someone else's property?
- Under what conditions might you be able to use lethal force?

# 5
# DEFINING THE MISSION & IDENTIFYING CRITICAL ASSETS

The first step, and possibly most important is to define your Mission. The Mission drives every decision you will make from there on. The Mission information will significantly shape how you identify Targets, assign risk, create training programs, make tactical decisions and assign specific posts for your security functions.

What is your Mission? Is it to protect an individual? Is it to protect their family? Is it to protect their house? Is it to protect company employees? The Mission will define the Assets that need protection.

Presumably, your Mission as an Executive Protection Agent is to protect an identified Asset and most of the time that Asset is some type of VIP.

If there is no identified Mission you need to ask questions about the Mission. Sometimes the Mission is obvious; as in protecting a person. But sometimes it is not about a person. You may be protecting a thing. For discussion sake, let's look at one hypothetical example.

**Defining The Mission**
Company XYZ makes a widget. Their Mission statement: "To manufacture the highest quality widget on the market at competitive prices in order to enhance the customer's life." They reportedly have a secret, proprietary formula for the widget that gives them the edge in the marketplace. If this formula were to get into the hands of the competition there would be significant loss to XYZ, as they are the only one in the marketplace offering the widget.

We can agree that this formula is what needs to be protected. It is the critical Asset. It is critical to the success of XYZ. This company can suffer losses to other assets without a significant loss of Mission. If the receptionist or CEO is killed it may be tragic but it will not create significant loss to XYZ, because it is all about the widget. Unless the CEO's or receptionist's abilities are as important as the proprietary formula – the CEO and receptionist can be replaced. This may sound a bit cold and impersonal, and this discussion with decision-makers may be difficult, but the discussion needs to take place.

If you were hired to protect the XYZ's widget, here are some of the questions you might be asking about the proprietary formula.

- Where does this proprietary formula go?
- Where is it stored?
- Who has access to it?
- Who actually manufactures the widget?
- To what degree is this formula already protected?
- Do we need to look at IT solutions?

Let's change the scenario. This time it is the same company, same widget and same Mission statement *but* no proprietary formula. Company XYZ sells the most widgets in the world because of the strong recognition of the CEO with the product and his brilliant marketing strategies and *not* because of some proprietary formula. This time it is the CEO who is identified as the critical Asset; which if degraded or destroyed, will seriously affect the Mission of XYZ. In this scenario the focus of protection shifts to a person; the CEO. You would want to know everything you could about the CEO's locations, patterns of behavior, family members, how he/she drives to work, etc. – because that is where the protection resources are going to be focused.

Finally, let's change the scenario one more time. This time it is the same company, same widget and same Mission statement with no proprietary formula. The administrators and decision-makers at XYZ identify their employees as the key to the success of the widget, explaining to you that the employees have been hand-selected and groomed over the years and they are irreplaceable. Now you have to figure out how to protect those employees and direct your resources there.

Get it?

Even if there is a clear Mission you still must have a discussion to identify what the critical Assets are; as defined by those assets which if compromised, degraded or destroyed, will seriously disrupt the Mission. You must come to an agreement as to what the Mission is and what the critical Assets of the Mission are.

Here are some discussion themes that should help identify the Mission and its critical Assets.

- What is the Mission?
- What are the goals of the Mission?
- What are the critical Assets of the Mission?
- What Assets, which if compromised, degraded or destroyed, will seriously disrupt or destroy the Mission?
- What risks are acceptable and tolerable?
- What loss of life, loss of systems or loss of operations will be acceptable in context of the Mission?

These questions will help you identify the Assets and what it is that really needs to be protected.

If, for example, an organization determines they want all employees protected, it should be noted that not all employees are essential to the Mission in the context we consider it here. Example: A staff member who loses their life, although tragic, might be easily replaced. A CEO may not be easily replaced because the CEO commands most of the vision and information required for the organization to accomplish its Mission. This is hypothetical and may or may not be the case with the organization you are dealing with.

Conversely, the CEO of a franchise operation might easily be replaced, but the loss of the entire franchise business plan might result in collapse of the whole franchise operation.

For most Executive Protection functions, the Mission seems simple. It is to make sure the person you are protecting does not suffer harm. This seems easy enough but it is also very short-sighted. There is much more to consider that goes far beyond physically escorting a person from point A to point B.

## A Quick Explanation

I wrote this book with the intention of giving the reader a very detailed overview of what Executive Protection is all about. It is written in a manner that should accomplish just that. If you just read this book and do nothing else, you should have a good idea of what Executive Protection is all about.

Yet, it is often helpful to connect principles to something concrete and real; something in real life. If you have been involved in Executive Protection work I would suggest you draw upon your personal experiences as you consider the principles throughout the book.

Many readers, however, have never worked an Executive Protection function so they will have little to refer to. For those readers, let me introduce you to Mr. Tommy Santos. By thinking about Mr. Santos you will have something "real" to apply these principles to.

## Meet Tommy Santos

You have been recruited to coordinate the personal security of Mr. Tommy Santos, who is a bestselling author and conservative radio talk show host of a popular syndicated program.

- Mr. Santos has a strong passion for conservative values.
- Mr. Santos has accepted a public speaking engagement at the shopping mall in your city.
- Mr. Santos may or may not bring his wife to this event.
- Mr. Santos's presentation will be conducted in the main lobby or largest public area in the mall. His presentation is expected to be ½ hour.
- After his presentation there will be a Meet and Greet with the public for 1 hour, in the form of a book signing table Mr. Santos will be at.
- Following the book signing, there will be a short Question & Answer session with the Press. Press coverage is expected at the event.
- Mr. Santos has received threats from people who strongly disagree with his values, vision and politics. Most of these threats have been investigated to a moderate degree and have been determined to be of low risk – mostly people venting their disagreement in anger. There have been several threats that are being taken seriously by his staff, and the people responsible for those threats have not been identified by law enforcement officials.

## Taking It To The Next Level

EP Agents are often tasked to protect people without adequate information – at least as far as they are concerned, and far too often they have no ability to accomplish advance work whereby they are visiting the location of an Executive Protection event ahead of time to look for risks. This can be very frustrating for the Agent, but it is also more usual than unusual. In this context and using the principles you have read so far in this book, to the best of your ability answer the following questions about Mr. Santos.

- What is the Mission?
- What are the goals of the Mission?
- What are the critical Assets of the Mission?
- What Assets, which if compromised, degraded or destroyed, will seriously disrupt or destroy the Mission?
- What risks are acceptable and tolerable?
- What loss of life, loss of systems or loss of operations will be acceptable in the context of the Mission?

If it will help to visualize this, visit your local Mall and just walk through it, locating the main public area where "Mr. Santos" will be speaking.

**Note:** Some readers might find it helpful to visit their local mall to visualize or otherwise assist them in more fully understanding some of the principles presented in this book. Many malls in the United States added extensive surveillance post 9/11. If you are approached by security personnel you should be forthright, respectful and honest about what you are doing.

# 6
# THE ASSET SURVEY

There is a tendency for new EP Agents to believe they should receive anything and everything they ask for from the event planner that hires them, the organization that wants their protection or the person they are protecting. You don't always get what you want and usually don't get something you think you really need. It is common to receive a lot less than what you ask for. This can cause conflict and is a source of frustration for the EP Agent. It can be a set-up for an adverse relationship with the people who hired you. This is not how you want to start a professional relationship. Remember that you have been retained to *serve* the people who are paying you. They are not there to *serve* you.

Remember the earlier reference to ballet? This is where it begins. How can you effectively protect a person who will not give you all the information you think you need to provide great protection? You must use tact and social grace when you are attempting to gather this information. Ultimately, you must accept what you are given and do the best with what you receive.

The bottom line with any protection detail is that you can always recommend best practices, and you should. But those recommendations might be rejected and you should accept that. You should tactfully point out why you are making a particular recommendation but it may not always be accepted.

Several years ago there was a large event scheduled in which select Senators, representatives of Congress and VIP's from large corporations would be attending. I was asked by the person responsible for the security of this event to look at his overall plan. After sitting down and looking at it on paper, I asked him to walk me through the building and parking lot that this event was scheduled to take place. As we did this I discovered vulnerability. Knowing most attacks take place at arrival and departure areas near vehicles, I noticed that the arrival area for the VIPs attending this event had numerous vulnerabilities. There were multiple roof-tops (potential snipers) nearby and the actual entrance into the building required the arriving VIPs to walk directly through a large public seating area. Instead, only 30 yards away, I found another entry into the building. The view of this entry from most of the rooftops would be partially obscured by a huge generator. This entry led to a secured ballroom. The hallway from this secured ballroom to the secure VIP holding area would require very little contact with the public except for about 20 yards between two doors. This entry was clearly a better choice for VIP safety. My suggestion to use this new entry and route for arriving VIPs was rejected by one of the hosts of the event, because; "I am *not* going to have these VIPs come through a locked-down ballroom. And besides, the Press won't be able to take pictures of them if we have them come in that way."

This is the type of conflict that can arise between the EP Agent and event planners, hosts, directors, handlers and a lot of other people that hover around VIPs. You can, and should tactfully point out that safety will be enhanced by using your recommendations but you ultimately have to accept whatever limitations are put on you; and preferably with a smile on your face. As an EP Agent, and particularly as someone who is coordinating the protection, you need to get this ingrained into your head immediately.

What we are talking about here is very different than an imminent threat. An imminent threat requires no explanation to anyone, just immediate action on your part. What we are discussing in this chapter is primarily occurring in the planning stages of a protection detail.

**The Asset Survey**
In planning any protection detail, you must first gather relevant information about whom or what it is that needs protection. Although there are many names for it, I call this an Asset Survey. It is information that is normally collected from the organization that is retaining your services, or an administrative assistant of the VIP or the event planner. It may come directly through a meeting with the VIP.

The amount of information you receive will vary in degrees of accuracy and relevance. It is recommended that you get as much information as possible knowing you may not receive everything you ask for.

All information should be kept confidential and your clients should be assured of this. The reason you are gathering it is simple; the more information you have about someone – the easier it is to protect them. By knowing these details you are better able to assess risk and allocate resources. The information you are gathering about them is considered very personal in nature. This particular Survey is arranged for protecting a person. If the Asset is a location or a thing, the Survey should be modified.

General Information
- Dates of assignment.
- How many people are being protected on this assignment?
- Length of assignment.
- Do you prefer armed or unarmed protection?
- Is 24-hour coverage required?
- What is the purpose of the visit?

Personal Information
- Name.
- Preferred Nickname or Alias.
- Address.
- Phone Numbers.
- Key Staff & Phone Numbers.
- Height.
- Weight.
- Facial Hair.
- Glasses.
- Light / Medium / Heavy Build
- Age.
- Specific Occupation.

Travel
- Does the assignment require travel?
- Purpose of travel.
- Please provide an itinerary.

Personal Interests
- Favorite food.
- Favorite beverage.
- Leisure activities.
- Medical issues and condition.
- Blood type.
- Allergies.
- Non-prescription drug preference.
- Dietary restrictions.
- Addictions.

Risk Information
- Social / Professional / Political / Religious Associations
- Specific threats or suspicious activity within the last year.
- Have you required Protection Services in the past?
- If yes, how frequently, why and with what firm's assistance?
- Are you licensed to carry a firearm, and if yes, will you be carrying one on this assignment?
- Please list the number and names of those who are licensed and will be carrying firearms.
- Have you or anyone in your immediate sphere of influence been involved in activity of any nature, which would give rise to threats (founded or otherwise) or avenues of extortion? Examples include drug use, gambling addictions or fetish lifestyles.
- What threat or source of extortion risk could you or any member of your sphere of influence represent to someone else?
- Do you have any reason to believe anyone within your sphere of influence holds any beliefs or values in areas of concern to them, which differ dramatically from your own? Examples include abortion, animal rights, politics, gay rights, etc.
- Have you ever noticed any gesture, comment or action to indicate someone had more than a normal level of envy or admiration for your social status?
- Have you or anyone in your immediate sphere of influence been involved, voluntarily or otherwise in any form of criminal activity?
- Is there anything else you think is important for us to know?

## Taking It To The Next Level

What follows is the completed Asset Survey for Tommy Santos that you have received from his administrative assistant. Look through it. If you received this information as an EP Agent, would you want to know anything else about him? What else might you want to know?

Asset Survey for Mr. Tommy Santos

- How many people are being protected on this assignment? Tommy Santos and possibly his wife; Grace.
- Length of assignment: From arrival at the airport until return to airport.
- Do you prefer armed or unarmed protection? No preference.
- Is 24-hour coverage required? No; just event and transportation from and back to airport for both inbound and outbound flights.
- What is the purpose of the visit? Speaking engagement at mall & book signing.
- Name: Tommy Santos
- Preferred Nickname or Alias: Tommy
- Address: 1657 Torway Drive, San Diego, CA 92139
- Phone Numbers: His administrative assistant is Tonya Peters and can be reached at xxx-xxx-xxxx. Her email address is: xxx@xxx.org
- Key Staff & Phone Numbers: see above
- Height: 6' – 0"
- Weight: 190
- Facial Hair: Mustache
- Glasses? Reading only
- Build: Light / Medium / Heavy Build
- Age: 43
- Occupation: Radio talk show host and author; professional speaker.
- Does the assignment require travel? Pick Mr. Santos up from airport and transport him to the Mall for speaking, book signing and Q&A with Press. After, return Mr. Santos to airport.
- Purpose of Travel: Same as above.
- Itinerary: Arrive airport at 4pm. Arrive Mall by 5pm. He will meet privately with event hosts. Speak, book signing and Q&A from 6pm – 9pm. Return to airport by 10pm for return flight.
- Favorite food: Steak
- Favorite beverage: Vitamin Water
- Leisure activities: Sports & Exercise
- Medical issues and condition: Seasonal allergies

- Blood type: Type O
- Allergies: Seasonal pollen.
- Non-prescription drug preference: Sudafed
- Dietary restrictions: None
- Addictions: None
- Other Risk Information: Conservative Catholic. Multiple letters and emails received daily in disagreement to his views. Several threats have been investigated by police and found to be "unsubstantiated" – people just venting and blowing off rather than a serious, credible threat. There have been several specific letters that Law Enforcement officials believe are from the same person in which the person is threatening to attack Mr. Santos in public, so "the world can see what a fraud you are". These letters are anonymous and are post-marked in Rawlings, Wyoming. There are no further leads.
- Have you required Protection Services in the past? Yes, for all public events.
- If yes, how frequently, why and with what company's assistance? We use local protection services whenever possible.
- Are you licensed to carry a firearm, and if yes, will you be carrying one on this assignment? Mr. Santos is a handgun permit holder in California due to the threats on his life. He does not travel armed out of state.
- Please list the number and names of those who are licensed and will be carrying firearms. No one traveling with Mr. Santos will be armed.
- Have you or anyone in your immediate sphere of influence been involved in activity of any nature, which would give rise to threats (founded or otherwise) or avenues of extortion? No.
- What threat or source of extortion risk could you or any member of your sphere of influence represent to someone else? As a well-known Conservative who has written several best-selling books and is heard by millions of people a day on his radio program, Mr. Santos is considered a target for all sorts of schemes.
- Do you have any reason to believe anyone within your sphere of influence holds any     beliefs or values in areas of concern to them, which differ dramatically from your own? Most of the people who work for Mr. Santos' organization are like-minded people.
- Have you ever noticed any gesture, comment or action to indicate someone had more than a normal level of envy or admiration for your social stature? Mr. Santos receives many emails and letters that range from supporters giving legitimate thanks to women sending him their underwear, and everything in between.

- Have you or anyone in your immediate sphere of influence been involved, voluntarily or otherwise in any form of criminal activity? No.
- Is there any else you think is important for us to know? Tommy's half-brother, Chuck Norgren, has been institutionalized several times with diagnosed mental illness. He has had episodes, when he is not taking his medication, of delusions where he believes that Tommy is the anti-Christ. Once, he attempted to break into Mr. Santos residence. The alarm was tripped and he was apprehended in the house by responding law enforcement and security personnel. When Mr. Norgren was taken into custody he was armed with a handgun, knife and a small container of anti-freeze. It is presumed that Mr. Norgren intended to kill Mr. Santos by putting the anti-freeze into a beverage in the residence, intending Mr. Santos to drink it. When Mr. Norgren is taking his medication, he is supportive of Mr. Santos and the men have a cordial relationship.

# 7
# IDENTIFY PRIMARY THREATS & DEFINE THE ADVERSARY

Thus far, you have defined the Mission and identified the critical Assets that need protection. In this chapter we ask the question; what does the Asset need to be protected from? By answering this question you will identify Targets requiring advance planning. We do this in order to help you determine what actually needs attention and resources. This process will help you focus on realistic potential risks rather than the traditional all-encompassing "protect-them-from-everything" shotgun approach that many Executive Protection Agents use. The answer to these next questions will come from information you have already gathered.

There are several categories that anyone wanting to do harm to another can fit into and these categories cover the full range of assaultive behavior. Which of the following Threat Groups have the greatest motivation to disrupt or destroy the Mission - by means of attacking your identified critical Assets?

## Threats from People
Military Action: Generally, the goal is some type or coup or takeover. These acts are usually motivated by ideological political or philosophical opposition.
Terrorism: Any act intended to cause death or serious bodily harm to civilians or non-combatants with the purpose of intimidating a population or compelling a government or an international organization to do or abstain from doing any act. These acts are usually motivated by ideological political or philosophical opposition.

Political Activism: A doctrine or policy which advocates active involvement as a means to achieve political or other goals. These acts are usually motivated by ideological political or philosophical opposition.

Crime: A type of behavior that is has been defined by the state, as deserving of punishment which usually includes imprisonment. Criminal acts usually carry an economic motivation for personal financial gain.

Mental Illness or Instability: Various disorders in which a person's thoughts, emotions or behavior are so abnormal as to cause suffering to himself, herself or other people. The motivation within this category is usually personal – with a desire for revenge, sabotage, retribution or some other intense personal agenda.

Insiders: Insiders are usually disgruntled, blackmailed or coerced employees. Most Insiders have some type of affiliation or relationship with the Asset that allows them access to places and things an outsider would not. They often work in collusion with the type of people listed above.

The underlying motivations within these categories are important, because if you can remove someone's motivation – or change it - you can usually influence behavior.

There can also be unexpected threats from some type of Man Made Hazard. These things just happen sometimes and are not necessarily a directed attack toward the identified critical Asset. They are, however, things you should prepare for – but only after you have addressed and/or eliminated Threats from People.

**Threats from Man Made Hazard**
- Bomb
- Power Failure
- Fire
- Civil Disturbance / Riot
- Robbery
- Hostage
- Assault
- Medical
- Car Accident
- Explosion
- Chemical Leak or Spill / Engineering Disaster (i.e. bridge collapse)

Additionally, there can be Threats from Nature. These are also things you should consider preparing for – but only after you have addressed and/or eliminated Threats from People & Threats from Man Made Hazards.

## Threats from Nature
- Earthquake
- Tsunami
- Flood
- Volcanic Eruption
- Economic Collapse
- Landslide or Mudslide
- Wildfire
- Weather: Heat, Cold, Thunderstorm, Hail, Hurricane, Tornado, Snow
- Pandemic & Infectious Disease
- Avalanche
- Drought
- Famine
- Impact Event (i.e. meteor)
- Sink Hole
- Solar Flare (present danger to satellites, communication systems, power grid systems through electromagnetic radiation)
- Storm Surge

It is possible that Threats from Nature or Threats from Man Made Hazards could be your primary consideration depending on the identified critical Assets. Let's look at a few examples.

If the identified critical Asset is a historic building that sits on a flood plain, your primary threat may be flooding.

Let's assume you have been retained to help a service business identify and protect their critical Assets. There are no proprietary formulas, no manufacturing and no products. This business does well but is located in a geographic area where there are frequent wildfires. You have helped them identify the actual workplace as one of their critical Assets, due to the IT system and the files on employee computer hard drives. Outside of the obvious, which is backing up all computer file information at a remote site, you have determined wildfire is their greatest Threat.

## Taking It To The Next Level

At this point you should begin to understand how to look at protection from an Executive Protection Agent's view, and in particular, an Executive Protection Administrator's perspective.

It should be clear that in order to provide good protection you need to define your Mission, identify your critical Assets and find out as much about those Assets as possible. Once you have done this you can see that by identifying the primary threat to your Asset, you have a good idea of what resources you need to acquire that will be effective in mitigating the risks that come with that identified threat.

Let's try and apply this to "Mr. Santos". It seems clear that his greatest threat is going to come from People Groups. Let common sense prevail; a Military Coup is not something Mr. Santos needs to worry about.

Which groups of people represent the greatest Threat to Mr. Santos?

Motivation is important because it drives behavior. If you can change someone's motivation, you may change their behavior. For *each* people group you identified as being a threat to Mr. Santos, what are the likely motivations of them?

For *each* people group you identified, what are the potential goals of the Adversary?

# 8
# DEFINING THE ADVERSARY'S METHOD OF OPERATION

Remember in a previous chapter I suggested you gather as much information as possible about the Asset you are protecting? In the same respect, once you have identified the most likely Threat (remember those Threats from People, Man Made Hazards and Threats from Nature?) you should gather Protective Intelligence about that Threat to make further decisions about what resources you will need to protect the Asset and how you will use them.

Gathering Protective Intelligence is the acquisition, maintenance, analysis and investigation of information regarding your Threat. That information is used with an emphasis on prevention. Although Protective Intelligence deals primarily with terrorist groups, criminal groups, social change and instability, and threats from individuals – it could also apply to the characteristics of a tornado if a tornado is your primary Threat.

The reason for conducting Protective Intelligence is to gather, evaluate and disseminate information that is directly relevant to the Threat and the immediate and future security of the Asset or Principal. The collection of intelligence must be directed, controlled and coordinated.

Liaisons with local, regional, national and military agencies are helpful. Other sources include local police agencies, government agencies, relatives, co-workers, visitors, all media sources, foreign intelligence and law enforcement. If you have already identified the likely Adversary, collecting Protective Intelligence is more productive because you already have a focus on what type of intelligence you need to obtain.

The type of information sought is Who, What, Where, When and Why. Then, look at Who again. Essentially, you are trying to determine what the identified Threat might present as a potential problem to your Asset.

Let's consider one hypothetical example using the radical arm of the PETA organization.

Your Asset (or the organization that has retained your services) has received numerous threatening letters complaining of something they have done in relation to animals. We know there are political activist groups capable of criminal acts or disruption based on historical data. PETA (People for the Ethical Treatment of Animals) purposely targets places, people and events of social meaning; looking for a way seize the headlines or to create their own headlines. PETA has over 1 million members worldwide and no shortage of funding. Some of their tactics include:

- Putting up billboards close to an organization with the daily number of animals affected by the organization.
- Bombarding the organization with demand letters.
- Flooding the organization's website with fake accounts, hate mail or spam.
- Sending meat to or dumping meat at the organization headquarters.
- Sponsoring a meat-free barbeque or chili cook-off near the organization.
- Throwing red paint and animal carcasses at employees.

So, from my brief review of available information from media sources we can see that radical environmental and animal rights groups have claimed responsibility for a large number of crimes and acts of terrorism, including arson, bombings, vandalism and harassment.

As I conduct Protective Intelligence about PETA it is helpful for me to focus on what their usual Method of Operation is; some of which are listed above.

In this case, I identified my most likely Threat as coming from a people group, not a man made hazard and not a threat from nature. Within that people group there are Trained Military Personnel, Terrorists, Political Activists & Extremists, Criminals or people with significant Mental Health issues. Since there were already threat letters from PETA, I would use whatever resources are available to educate myself and understand PETA's methods and motivation. By doing this I know how to prepare for a protection event or detail with this organization.

I am looking for both general and specific information regarding the characteristics of my identified threat. I am looking for the common Methods of Operation and common behavioral traits.

**Framing the Method of Operation**
There are a limited number of ways people can physically attack others. They are:

- 1-2 people (or more) with no tools or weapons.
- 1-2 people with hand and power tools.
- 1-2 people with hand and power tools and hand weapons.
- 1-2 people with tools, hand weapons and a suitcase bomb.
- Car bomb.
- Truck bomb.
- Chemical or biological weapons.

When you consider these choices, first look at the common characteristics and behavioral traits you have discovered for the particular threat you have identified. In the PETA example you would try to determine if the letters that the organization received are from an organized activist group or a lone individual. Knowing this allows you to further define what it is you need to prepare for. If you have determined there is a greater likelihood that a lone individual is sending the letters rather than an organized group, you would probably be preparing to deal with someone who may exhibit mental health issues and instability. The preparations and planning for a lone individual with mental health issues is different than for an organized political activist group.

Additionally, PETA does not generally use car or truck bombs as part of their tactics, but a lone individual with mental health issues might consider using explosives. Determine the methods and weapons *most likely* available to the identified Adversary.

When doing so, also consider what type of access the Adversary might have to equipment, specialized knowledge, technical experience, transportation or Insiders within the organization. The likely Method of Operation of the Adversary is predicated on what is available to the Adversary and what levels of security are in place.

Example: In the PETA scenario, if there are multiple unsecured entrances to the building of the organization that has received the letters, there is great opportunity for the Adversary to enter the building and carry out whatever they have planned.

Contrast this to the same organization that has a fenced parking lot with cameras. All the entrances are locked and alarmed except the main entrance where a guard is posted and identification is required. All employee bags are checked and all visitors walk through a metal detector.

This second scenario eliminates a number of the methods available to the Adversary. This level of security may eliminate or mitigate the opportunity of hand and power tools, hand weapons or a suitcase bomb. In this scenario the Adversary has to adapt his Method of Operation to fit the level of security. Levels of security may eliminate or mitigate opportunity and Methods of Operation.

Another factor to consider is the availability of specific weapons to the Adversary. How difficult is it for the Adversary to gain possession of chemical & biological weapons, or the ingredients necessary to build a suitcase bomb? These factors are based on the geographic location of the Adversary and the sophistication of knowledge available to the Adversary.

## Inside the Attack

Just 2 Seconds: Using Time And Space To Defeat Assassins was written by Gavin De Becker, Tom Taylor & Jeff Marquart. Read it. There is valuable information in their research as it applies to Executive Protection. Their work validates what many of us in this business have known for years.

To begin to put violent behavior into the proper context for Executive Protection Agents, it helps to know what happens in real-life. Why? Because your assignment may (and probably will) take you into public places in which crimes still take place and people are still robbed, beaten and assaulted – even though these acts may have nothing to do directly with your presence or the presence of your Asset.

Additionally, there is valuable information that any person you might be protecting should know. Not just for them but for their family members and loved ones as well. After all, you may not always be with them and EP Agents may not always be around them. By virtue of understanding some of the basic dynamics of violent crime, these people can become an ally rather than a hindrance in the event of an attack.

### National Violence Statistics

After studying the statistics available from the Bureau of Justice Statistics National Crime Victimization Survey, there are some fairly solid conclusions we can come to.

- You are far more likely to be the victim of a robbery than an assault with injury or sexual assault. However, robberies have violent characteristics.

- The average duration of a typical violent encounter is less than 2 minutes.

- 53% of incidents of violent crime occurred during the day between 6AM-6PM.

- The location of about a quarter of incidents of violent crime was at or near the victim's home. Among common locales for violent crimes was on streets other than those near the victim's home (19%), at school (12%), or at a commercial establishment (8%).

- For violent crime, about half occurred within a mile from home and 76% within five miles. Only 4% of victims of violent crime reported that the crime took place more than fifty miles from their home.

- Of victims of violent crime, 22% were involved in some form of leisure activity away from home at the time of their victimization, 22% said they were at home, and another 20% said they were at work or traveling to or from work when the crime occurred.

- In 24% of the incidents of violent crime, a weapon was present.

- Homicides are most often committed with guns, especially handguns. About 55% of homicides are committed with handguns, 16% with other guns, 14% with knives, 5% with blunt objects, and 11% with other weapons.

- An examination of the supplemental data regarding the type of weapons offenders used in the commission of a robbery revealed that assailants relied on strong-arm tactics in 41.1 percent of robberies and they employed firearms in 40.6 percent of robberies. Offenders used knives or other cutting instruments in 8.9 percent of these crimes. In the remaining 9.4 percent of robberies, the offenders used other types of weapons.

- Offenders had or used a weapon in 48% of all robberies, compared with 22% of all aggravated assaults.

For Sexual Assault
- Offenders had or used a weapon in 7% of all rapes/sexual assaults.
- Most often a threatening presence and verbal threats were used to maintain control over the victim.
- Minimal or no force was used in the majority of instances.
- The victims physically, passively or verbally resisted the rapists in slightly over 50% of the offenses.

- The most common offender reaction to resistance was to verbally threaten the victim.

It would make sense then, that in regards to personal safety, practical self defense - based on research - should include the following:
- Techniques that will keep the Adversary away from us.
- Techniques that will allow escape should the Adversary attempt to control us through strong-arm tactics.
- In the event a weapon is used (24% of incidents), techniques to disarm the Adversary's attempts to control us with the use of a gun, knife or blunt object - so we can escape.

**Public Attacks**
Attacks on VIPs are somewhat different in their characteristics and nature, and this data really depends on whether you are in the United States or overseas. Within the United States most public attacks are over within 5 seconds. That may seem like very little time, but your brain is able to process a lot of information within that time frame.

I was escorting a VIP to his vehicle after an event in which he spoke to a large audience on a very cold winter day. We exited through a main public entrance that consisted of a long bank of glass doors, like you might see on any corporate building. Just outside of these doors was a large metal landing and then several steps down to a parking lot. As I walked beside him I observed a man and a woman walking towards us from about 25 feet away. Within several seconds this is what went through my head.
- Why were these people walking into this building instead of away from it? The event was over.
- The man's coat was open on a sub zero day. This seemed odd.
- The man's hand was inside his coat near his armpit. This is a classic reach to un-holster a handgun from a shoulder holster.
- The man and woman were walking directly toward my VIP; even though there was ample room on this staircase, which was about 15-yards wide.
- As I began to reach for my firearm, which was located at my waistline, I wondered how accurate my shooting would be due to my thumb, which was in a splint from a training injury.
- The public was everywhere. There were people on the steps, in the parking lot and behind me – leaving the building. I wondered about collateral damage to innocent people if I had to shoot.
- I positioned myself in front of my VIP and above the approaching man and woman on the steps. I determined that if this man did draw

a weapon, I would be able to leap on him from a slightly advantageous position above him while also blocking a direct shot to the VIP.

- I was confident that if this man began to pull a gun out from his coat, I would be able to intervene effectively before the gun cleared his jacket.
- Focusing on the right hand inside his jacket I knew he would have to swing the gun completely across his body to take a shot at my VIP.
- As he began to withdraw his hand from his coat, I saw a black object in his hand.
- I was now ready to leap on this man from about 6 feet away. All I needed was confirmation that he was drawing a weapon.

The man pulled out a small portfolio about the size of an address book. It was black in color. He smiled and said hello to my VIP and then continued into the building with the woman who accompanied him. All that in several seconds. Several principles emerge.

If the EP Agent is in a good position they can almost always prevail. I will reiterate this throughout the book. In the example I just used, I had to be in a position to observe things that seemed odd and I had to be in a position to be able to react to those things effectively.

Adversaries have a lot of chances to fail, but only one chance to succeed – and that opportunity requires certain variables. Just like a criminal needs certain things from "good" victims to commit their crimes, Adversaries will strike when they think they have the best chance of success. Adversaries know they will not get another chance.

Perception of how well a Principal is protected and the Adversary's ability to get to them is everything! Therefore, EP Agents *must* project a professional image. For most public attackers, it is all about the act – not the specific target. You want Perception to speak loudly to the potential Adversary, telling them to go pick another Principal. The lack of professionalism in EP work is inexcusable. Few prospective Agents will ever actually work in the field and even fewer will do the work with excellence.

It is all about distance, because distance creates time and time has a direct relationship to Action vs. Reaction. You want extra time – to think and react. When the EP Agent is 15-feet from an attacking Adversary, the Adversary is likely to prevail. At 7 feet from the Adversary it is a close contest. But, if you are within arms-reach of an attacking Adversary there is no contest at all – the EP Agent wins. Sadly, De Becker's research indicates if the Agent is more than 25 feet from the *Principal* (not the Adversary) – the Agent will have *no* impact on the outcome of an attack.

In the US most attackers are lone Adversaries (87%). Outside the US this figure is inverted where 71% of attacks come from multiple Adversaries.

If you are working in the US, look for individuals who are behaving inappropriately. This word, "inappropriate" is the best measure of unusual behavior. In the example I used on that cold winter day, it seemed odd and inappropriate for this couple to be walking into a building after an event in which everyone else was leaving, and that the man's coat was open on a day when the temperatures were below zero.

US attacks are almost evenly divided between indoors and outdoors.

71% of attacks come using firearms – with handguns being used 51% of the time and long guns being used 20%. The reverse is true outside the US – where long guns are used more often. You should know how to disarm an Adversary who has a firearm.

Most attacks in the US come from less than 25 feet away from the Principal. This is true outside the US as well, even though long guns (rifles) are used more often. Creating space buffers of more than 25 feet between the Principal and the public almost guarantees the Principal's safety.

Better and more available Emergency Medical Services in the US reduces the death and injury rate. Do you know where the closest hospital is? Are EMS personnel on stand-by?

Bombs are about as successful as often as they fail. They fail 57% of the time. Bombs and IED's are a whole different deal. The primary things you can do as an EP Agent to reduce the risk of bombs and IEDs are to complete advance work that includes a focus on unusual and suspicious packages. In addition, travel in a *fully* armored car. Change driving routes and schedules frequently.

Attacks occur most frequently (64%) around the Principal's vehicle and are 77% successful. Beware of arrivals and departures.

Once an attack begins, *always* move the Principal toward safety.

## A Few More Tidbits

Specifically, 85% of *firearm and knife attacks* were over in less than 5 seconds. Weapons used in public attacks are as follows:

- 49% are handguns.
- 29% are long rifles.
- 15% are explosive devices, but 70% of those are delivered through the mail.
- 5% are knives and edged weapons.
- 2% are fists.
- Common location of attacks:
- 57% occurred at the Principal's office or home.
- 28% occurred while the Principal was moving to or from a building or vehicle.
- 14% occurred while the Principal was in the vehicle.
- A total of 42% of attacks are in or around vehicles and/or arrival departure situations.

## Most Important

The number one thing an EP Agent can do before a protection event is effective site advance, and positioning other Agents using these statistics as a guide. Create space between the Principal and other people. Close the space between EP Agents and potential Adversaries. The number one thing an EP Agent can do *during* a protective detail is to stay focused in the moment.

The best Executive Protection training comes through simulations using the most probable scenarios. Most Adversaries have to use fine and complex motor skills to complete an attack, while most EP Agents can use gross motor skills to deflect or intervene in an attack. For example, a bullet fired from 25 feet away can be thrown off by more than 6 feet if an EP Agent can redirect the angle of a shot by one inch.

Positioning, Perception and Performance is everything.

## Taking It To The Next Level

Let's try and apply this chapter to Mr. Santos. Within the People Group you have identified the most likely Adversary/Adversaries. Within *those* groups, identify the most likely Methods of Operation. This would be based on Protective Intelligence that you have gathered.

- 1-2 people with no tools or weapons.
- 1-2 people with hand and power tools.
- 1-2 people with hand and power tools and hand weapons.
- 1-2 people with tools, hand weapons and a suitcase bomb.
- Car bomb.
- Truck bomb.
- Chemical or biological weapons.
- An insider.
- Other:

# 9
# COMMON DENOMINATORS OF ATTACKERS

The number one indicator that an attack is going to take place is the "tell". A "tell" is a term commonly associated with playing poker in which a player's behavior or demeanor is a clue to what that player is holding in their hand. Other players feel like they gain some advantage if they can observe and understand those behaviors displayed by their opponents. In the same respect, most attackers give a "tell" prior to an attack. The EP Agent needs to know what "tells" to look for and then make decisions about how to deal with them.

Intuition is a hard-wired, genetic part of who we are. It is the "sixth sense", gut feeling, "funny" feeling or instinct. Call it what you will, but it should not be ignored or rationalized away. It is there for a reason. It is always working, even when you are asleep. It is a survival gift.

The biggest enemies of intuition are justification, rationalization and denial. Example: I awaken at 3:00am and hear noise in my basement. My justification, rationalization or denial says: "It must be the furnace making noise", when really it is a burglar rummaging through the house.

Victims, in post-crime interviews, often refer to a moment when their intuition was trying to tell them something and they justified it, rationalized it or denied it away. Example: Several years ago I was involved in a case in which a jilted husband, separated from his wife, suspected her of being unfaithful to him. In fact, his wife had a boyfriend and was attempting to keep it a secret.

The jilted husband hand-delivered a pipe bomb, in a toolbox, to his estranged wife's residence in the wee hours of the morning. She discovered it later that day on her front doorstep. In an interview I conducted with her several days later from her hospital bed, she advised me:

- She thought the package looked odd, due to it being wrapped in a reversed grocery paper bag, and having a return address on it she did not recognize.
- She called her boyfriend, who was at work, and advised him of the discovery.
- The boyfriend advised her to move the package to the back porch. This action indicated to me they both thought something was suspicious about the package.
- The boyfriend advised her to carefully remove the outer wrapping on the package. She did so and found a new red toolbox.
- Next, she attempted to open it, but reported the latches on the toolbox seemed tight.
- With the boyfriend still on the phone, they joked about it being a bomb from her estranged husband, but agreed he was not *that* crazy.
- Finally, they agreed she should use an outstretched rake handle to try and open the latch of the toolbox on the porch while she hid behind a portion of the back door – reaching out towards the toolbox.
- She managed to unlatch the tool box, which was spring-loaded. BOOM! She lost several fingers, was full of shrapnel, and the residence started on fire.

This is a perfect example of how justification, rationalization and denial got in the way of intuition. In this story Intuition was screaming. It's voice was silenced by the woman and her boyfriend working against it instead of paying attention to it. We found evidence of pipe bomb materials at the estranged husband's home and identified the store where he bought the toolbox. A warrant was issued. We discovered he had fled to Mexico.

Bottom Line: Pay attention to your intuition. It is trying to tell you something. The EP Agent's intuition is probably the thing that will detect the "tell". Don't ignore it.

Of course, once you do detect a "tell" you need to do something about it. Working on small protection teams or alone does not afford you the luxury of coming back to a discovered "tell" later – because by then it may be too late, or you may have missed your only chance to effectively intervene in an attack. The purpose of this chapter is two-fold. First, it provides a good example of how to gather Protective Intelligence. Please take note of the resources I have cited. These reports are all available from media sources. Although I am summarizing the key findings from them, and have spent a considerable part of my career studying violent behavior - looking for information and using that information to come to conclusions about your identified Adversary (or anything else you want to know about your protection detail) is what Protective Intelligence is all about.

Secondly, this chapter presents reliable information about Attackers. I have attempted to sift through a lot of information about Attackers and distill it into a reasonable list of characteristics that Attackers share.

The bullet points present reliable information from the indicated source, immediately followed by my comments, if appropriate, as to what practicality this information has for the EP Agent.

**First Resource: Former US Secret Service Psychologist**
It is the act and not the target, the destination, nor the journey that's important. The target is interchangeable. This theme is universally agreed upon in research and literature regarding Public Attackers and Assassins.

The common feature assassins share is the lack of healthy, intimate relationships. This fact is of little value to the EP Agent who is constantly on the move because they have no idea of the backgrounds of the people they are observing. It is of benefit to the Agent whose responsibilities include investigating inappropriate or odd communications towards the Principal, where there is focus on a particular individual.

Assassins do not fear going to jail; they fear they are going to fail. They are driven by a successful attack. The EP Agent just needs to reduce the chances of success to the point that the Adversary's perception is that he would be better off choosing another Principal to attack. Attackers share an ability belief that they can successfully accomplish a public attack. Without that belief they can do nothing, because perception is everything and it drives behavior.

Narcissism is the central feature of every assassin. Narcissism goes well-beyond selfishness or being somewhat self-absorbed. It is a diagnosable psychological condition. A true narcissist has little ability to empathize with anything other than what they think is important. People who do not get recognition in childhood seek it in adulthood. There is an attention-getting aspect to the attack.

There are 10 behaviors common to modern assassins. These are "tells". If you come across one in relation to your protection responsibilities you should investigate further.

- Displayed some mental disorder.
- Researched the target or victim.
- Created a diary, journal or record.
- Obtained a weapon.
- Communicated inappropriately with some public figure, though not necessarily the one attacked.
- Displayed an exaggerated idea of self.
- Random travel.
- Identified with a stalker or assassin.
- Had the ability to circumvent *ordinary* security. Note: This is why you need to be extraordinary.
- Made repeated approaches to some public figure.

This is why, in the planning stages, it is good to think about the most likely Adversary you might encounter and their primary methods of operation. In the planning stages of a protection detail it will be desirable to consider the perceptions of that primary Adversary you have identified, and then try to impact those perceptions in a manner that discourages an attack.

**Second Resource**
**Assassination in the United States: An Operational Study of Recent Assassins, Attackers, and Near-Lethal Approachers**
From the Journal of Forensic Sciences published in March 1999. This article was based on the Secret Service Exceptional Case Study Project. At that time the study was the first operational exploration of the thinking and behavior of 83 persons known to have attacked, or approached to attack, a prominent public official or public figure in the United States since 1949. The method of collecting data was exhaustive. In every case, the attack or near attack was the end result of an understandable and often discernible process of thinking and action.

Did you catch that part about "often discernible"? This is the "tell". The Key Findings of this report are:

- Ages ranged widely, from 16 to 73. There is no average, or profile age. Most were males.
- Often, they were well-educated. Almost half had attended some college education or graduated.

- Attackers and near attackers often had histories of mobility and transience.
- Most were described as social isolates. However, about 1/3 of the subjects did not appear to be, and were not described as social isolates.
- Many subjects had histories of harassing other persons.
- Most are known to have had histories of explosive, angry behavior, but only half of the subjects are known to have had histories of violent behavior.
- Few subjects had histories of arrests for violent crimes or for crimes that involved weapons.
- Few had ever been incarcerated in state or federal prisons before their public figure directed attack or near lethal approach.
- Most attackers and would-be attackers had histories of weapons use, but no formal weapons training.
- Most attackers had interest in militant/radical ideas and groups, but were not active members of such groups at the time of their attacks.
- Many attackers had histories of serious depression or despair.
- Many are known to have attempted to kill themselves, or known to have considered killing themselves at some point before their attack or near-lethal approach.
- Many subjects had previous contact with mental health professionals or care systems at some point in their lives before their attack or near-lethal approach. However, few indicated to mental health staff that they were considering attacking a public official or public figure.
- Few subjects had histories of command hallucinations.
- Relatively few subjects had histories of substance abuse, including alcohol.

All of this is interesting and is of some academic benefit, but unless you are in a position in which you are investigating inappropriate or odd communications from a potential Adversary towards the Principal, the information from this resource is of little or no benefit to the EP Agent who is working in the moment. What is useful here is that attackers seem to share some attributes that might present "tells" in certain social situations or interactions. The potential attacker who is a social isolate and has a tendency to harass other people or has a tendency towards explosive or angry behavior and is experiencing depression or despair – will interact differently with in social situations than people who are *not* experiencing these things. Often times, people with these attributes will exhibit behavior in a manner that seems odd or inappropriate; small things that your intuition might pick up on.

And what is the easiest way to make this determination? It is to engage that person of interest somehow; to interact with them; to look them in the eye, hear their tone of voice and watch their body language. And herein lays the importance of creating *some* type of interaction with a person of interest.

Although the general public likes to dismiss people who attack as "nuts" or "crazy", the fact is that most public attackers actually think that the attack is a solution to resolving some problem in their lives. Most often that problem is not rare, nor is it extreme. Their motives include gaining notoriety, righting a perceived wrong, producing political change, making money or achieving a special relationship with the Principal. In fact, most attackers used rational thought processes when considering and planning their attacks. This does not mean most attackers are not experiencing some psychological problems because clearly they are. But there is a big difference between psychological stressors which can lead any of us to some pretty strange thinking – and mental illness.

For the most part, you can deter these individuals through good protection habits and procedures, but there is almost one-third of public attackers also carry a "death-wish". In these cases the Adversary might try to attack a well-protected Principal *hoping* to get injured, killed or arrested.

Almost two-thirds of attackers are known to have made some threat about their targets in the days, weeks or months before their attack or near-lethal approach; either through comments or writing. These actions are "tells".

The major overall finding of this study is that most of these attacks are preventable – but you need to be in a position to observe these discernible behaviors that often precede an attack - and most EP Agents are not in that position. More often, the EP Agent meets this person in the midst of an attack.

### Third Resource - The Final Report and Findings of the Safe School Initiative: Implications for the Prevention of School Attacks in the United States

This report followed a three-year partnership between the U.S. Department of Education and the U.S. Secret Service. It examined the behavior and thinking of young people who commit acts of targeted violence in the nation's schools.

Incidents of targeted violence at school are rarely sudden, impulsive acts. However, since the time between the decision to attack and the actual event is unpredictable, intervention should be swift when a "tell" is discovered.

Prior to most incidents, others knew about the attacker's idea or plan to attack. In most cases those who knew were other kids and the information rarely made its way to an adult. Commonly, the information caused those who knew about it considerable concern. Therefore, environments need to be established that allow for the free-flow of this information.

Most attackers did not threaten their targets prior to advancing the attack. However, there were other "tells" present; threats or other details regarding the attack. There is a difference between expressing anger, which many of us do – and engaging in direct behavior that indicates intent, planning or preparation for an attack.

There is no accurate or useful profile of students who engaged in targeted school violence. Focus on behavior, not profiles.

Most attackers had problems coping with significant losses or personal failures. Many had considered or attempted suicide. Many attackers felt bullied, persecuted or injured by others prior to the attack. More than half of the attackers had revenge as a motive and almost three-quarters were known to hold a grievance prior to the attack. These types of behaviors in any setting amount to harassment and/or assault. Therefore, create environments where bullying is not acceptable. The lesson here is that the attacker's *perception* is one of some type of personal injustice or personal pain with little hope of addressing it successfully. Remember, people engage in conflict out of emotion; not logic. Always try to discover the emotion that is fueling the thinking. People are not nearly as complex as we like to make them. The fact is that perception precedes thought. A thought always precedes an impulse. An impulse precedes action, or behavior. This is why we make considerable efforts in shaping, forming and impacting people's perception. If you are an EP Agent you want the Adversary's perception to be affected by the plans you put around your Asset. You want them to go somewhere else to do their deed. As you move from perception toward behavior, it gets more difficult to intervene. Successful intervention into an attack begins at the "perception" stage.

Most attackers had access to and had used weapons prior to the attack. Two-thirds of attackers sourced the guns used in attacks from their own home or that of a relative. Therefore, any attempt to procure, access or use a weapon should be considered a red flag.

In most cases, the attacker acted alone.

Despite prompt law enforcement response, most shooting incidents were resolved before law enforcement authorities arrived on the scene. Other students or faculty stepped in, or the student stopped shooting or committed suicide. Remember that five-second window of an attack we talked about in Chapter 5? The average law enforcement response time in the United States is 6 minutes and 50 seconds.

## Common Denominators

When we look at a lot of the research available about people who are public attackers these common denominators are found.

Emotional

- Lack of healthy, intimate relationships. Most subjects had great difficulty building and maintaining consistent relationships in their lives. Social isolates.
- Narcissism. Displayed an exaggerated idea of self.
- Previous contact with mental health professionals. Mental disorder, but not diagnosed.
- Histories of explosive, angry behavior. Histories of harassing other persons.
- Histories of serious depression or despair. Attempted or considered suicide.
- Had problems coping with significant losses or personal failures. Difficulty coping with (normal) problems in their lives. The attack or near-lethal approach occurred after a period of downward spiral in their lives – most within the year before their attack.
- Felt bullied, persecuted or injured by others.

Cognitive

- Well educated.
- Interest (not membership) in militant/radical ideas and groups. Interest in previous assassination attempts.
- Identified with a stalker or assassin.
- Communicating to others or keeping a journal, diary or record about their thoughts and activities. Engaged in some behavior, prior to the incident, that caused others concern or indicated a need for help. Others knew about the attacker's idea or plan to attack. Others were involved in the attack in some capacity. The attacker was influenced or encouraged by others (whether the others knew it or not). In most cases, the attacker actually acted alone.
- Belief that they could accomplish the attack.
- Came to see an attack as a solution, or way out, of their problems.

Behavioral
- Rarely sudden, impulsive acts.
- Researched the target or victim. Made repeated approaches to the target or similar targets. Had the ability to circumvent ordinary security.
- Histories of weapons use. Obtained a weapon. Had access to and had used weapons prior to the attack.
- Communicated or exhibited inappropriate behavior with target.
- Selection of targets was influenced by several factors, including the potential attacker's motives, and found or perceived opportunities to attack.
- Group attackers generally planned with some care.
- Circumstantial and generally associated with Assassins are two traits: They traveled randomly and had histories of mobility and transience.

Motivation
- Subjects whose major motivation was to be killed or removed from society often chose a target that they saw as well protected.
- Conversely, a subject who does not wish – or is not prepared to risk death, might avoid a target known to be well protected.

**Taking It To The Next Level**
Conduct some basic research into the following people and compare your findings about these people to the attributes and characteristics presented in the last section of this chapter; Common Denominators.
- John Hinkley
- Oscar Ramiro Ortega-Hernandez
- Vladimir Arutyunian
- Francisco Martin Duran
- Lynnette "Squeaky" Fromme
- Samuel J. Byck
- Sirhan Sirhan
- Lee Harvey Oswald
- John Schrank
- John Wilkes Booth
- Richard Lawrence
- Mark David Chapman

# 10
# TARGET IDENTIFICATION

Several years ago I was retained by a businessman who had fled his native war-torn country when he was 17. He had come to the United States and pursued an education. After obtaining several degrees and working for a few other employers he started his own company which grew to be a very successful niche company for certain "widgets".

His basic issues were that within the last year;

- His boat had been torched.
- Windows at his home had been broken.
- The phone lines and security system lines at his home had been cut.
- He had been forced off of the road while driving to work.
- At a party attended by industry professionals he had been subtly threatened.
- On several occasions someone tried to break into his company headquarters.

I began to conduct an Asset Survey after determining the Mission was to protect him and that he was the critical Asset. Not only was he a gifted engineer and technician but he was also an imposing force. As the owner of this company he was very direct in his communications to his employees and even his top people seemed to be intimidated by him. I wondered if one of his own people was behind these actions just because of the way he treated them. After several meetings with him it became clear to me that other industry professionals were most likely responsible for these attacks – as he had quite openly challenged their methods of doing business and he was bucking the status quo. Looking at the Threat from People Groups, I decided that the most likely Adversary was some combination of the Terrorist, the Political Activist and the Criminal. It was clear that others were using simple criminal acts intended to produce fear in hopes that my client might change his business practices. Whoever it was, their Methods of Operation were already clear.

I completed a home protection survey of his residence. I brought in several attorneys to meet with him so that we might explore legal options. Although he had his own ideas who was behind these acts, he had no intention of involving law enforcement. He wanted to take care of this his way and we made sure his plan to resolve this was legal and above reproach. While his plan was taking shape I had the responsibility of keeping him safe. In order for me to do this I had to identify Targets; things that could be attacked by the Adversary which would put my client at risk.

## How To Identify Targets

The Mission is now defined. You have determined the critical Assets that need protection and where they are located. You have also determined what represents the greatest threat to your Asset. If this is a People Group you also know the Adversary's likely method of operation – because you have narrowed down the likely Adversary and conducted Protective Intelligence. Next, you will determine the likely Targets. Targets are different than Assets. *Targets are things, places, people, patterns, systems, etc. that, if destroyed, degraded or compromised, increase the vulnerability of the identified Asset.*

One of the easiest methods of determining Targets is to assume the mindset of the Adversary and their Methods of Operation, or whatever the identified primary threat is. If you know enough about the Asset, try to imagine where, when and how you can get to it and destroy it. To understand this more fully, let's go back to the example of company XYZ with the widget that I introduced in Chapter 5.

If the identified critical Asset is the proprietary formula for the widget, good Targets might include, but are not limited to:
- The safe where the formula is stored.
- The IT system.
- The manufacturing plant.
- Anywhere else the formula might be.
- A person who knows the formula.

If the identified critical Asset is the CEO, good Targets might include, but are not limited to:

- The home of the CEO.
- The travel route of the CEO.
- The CEO's vehicle.
- The building or security system where the CEO's office is.
- The CEO parking area.
- The CEO's protection Agent or protection team.
- The family members of the CEO.

If the identified critical Assets are the employees, good Targets might include, but are not limited to:

- The parking lot.
- Entrances, exits and break areas.
- The building or security system where the employees are.
- The personal behavioral patterns of employees.
- The behavioral patterns of employees after they leave the office.

The following discussion questions will help in identifying Targets. Target Identification may involve Site Advance work in the field. Site Advance work requires going to the Target locations to accurately identify vulnerabilities.

The first question you should ask is; Where does the identified critical Asset "travel" and where is it located? A critical Asset may be identified as a person, a place or a thing. Think outside of the box. If one of the critical Assets is identified as a document locked in a safe, this answer is simple. You need to protect the safe and limit who has access to it.

What about a proprietary formula? It may be stored in a safe, stored on computers, travel across the internet and be at a manufacturing plant somewhere overseas. An Asset's travels and locations may be simple or complex.

Your identified Asset in this book is Mr. Santos, and perhaps his wife or other family members depending on whether they travel with him. Begin to ask these questions as you consider the selection of Targets. Targets can have multiple locations. Locations can have multiple Targets.

- Within the Asset's travels and locations where are the likeliest places for violent acts?
- Where is the likeliest location for death or critical injuries?
- Can anything that the Asset uses be sabotaged?

- Where are the vulnerabilities?
- Are there specific areas and/or equipment that could be attacked which would increase the Asset's vulnerability? How might an Adversary disable or destroy those areas or equipment? How many acts are required to achieve this? Example: Theft is usually a single act, but sabotage can be multiple acts.
- What risks are present that might jeopardize the Assets?
- What is the operational trade-off when deciding about risk? Example: If theft is a major problem but the decision-makers do not want to spend money on the implementation of a system to curtail theft, they must accept the consequences of the theft that is sure to continue.
- What protective measures are already in place to protect the Asset? Example: Let's assume both the CEO and the Sales & Marketing Vice President are identified as the critical Assets of an organization. They both have a security team or person that travels with them. This will reduce their risk and also affect your planning. There may be some procedures in place that add to, or detract from your ability to protect these identified Assets. Let's assume for a moment that the CEO and VP travel by private plane. This will reduce their overall risk because they will have less contact with the general public at a private airport. You should be looking at what procedures are already in place that add to, or detract from the identified Assets being protected.
- What will be the cost options? Is there a budget dedicated to these outcomes? How much reduction in risk can be funded? Example: Do you have a budget to rent a metal detector that everyone attending the event can walk through? Would something like this even be allowed?

**Site Advance**
A Site Advance consists of visiting the Targets you have identified and the places that your Asset is going to be. You do this ahead of time to discover vulnerabilities and risks. Depending on your status of employment, you may or may not have the luxury of conducting this type of field work. If you are protecting someone who travels a lot, it is unlikely you are going to be able to send an Agent or a team ahead of the Principal's itinerary unless you are working for someone with a very healthy budget.

If you are working a specific event or providing protection for a Principal who travels very little and frequents the same places, you should be able to accomplish Site Advance field work.

Preferably, you will conduct a Site Advance after you have determined the Targets. Targets are things, places, people, patterns, systems, etc. that, if destroyed, degraded or compromised, increase the vulnerability of – and the risks to – your Asset. Identifying Targets may seem obvious, as in the case of a public figure that requires protection or valuable artwork locked in a vault. In these scenarios the Target would be the public figure or the artwork, right?

Yes - but Target Identification goes deeper than this.

For example, your Principal may walk from his car to the building he works in every day covering a space of almost 100 yards. For our purposes here, let's assume the Principal owns this property. This space is not monitored. There are no gates, no guards, no cameras, no sensors and free access. It stands to reason that this space would be an excellent place for an Adversary to plan an attack. Therefore, this space becomes a vulnerability that must be addressed as part of Target Identification. This space *is* a Target because it is a place the Principal will be. This space, given free reign by an Adversary, will increase the risk to the Principal. In this example, if you consider *only* the Principal you may be tempted to provide a personal escort for them each day and leave it at that. How about having an EP Agent sweep the area each day before the Principal arrives? Or shutting the gates that are usually left open to public traffic in this area; or installing camera surveillance; or suggesting the Principal park in a more secure area? You must think beyond the obvious or you leave vulnerabilities unchecked.

Physical assets are usually a little easier to deal with because they have a tendency to travel less and stay in the same place for longer periods.

If you know what the Asset is, and where it is going - or where it is going to be located - you can begin to identify Targets. Once you have identified Targets, you could conduct Site Advance field work with the purpose of discovering vulnerabilities within those Targets.

To the degree possible and practical, there should be advance planning and observation of the routes and sites that will be used by, and visited by the Principal. These sites must be secured to an acceptable level. Preferably, you will do the Site Advance field work yourself or delegate it to someone on your team. This is not always possible or practical. If you are protecting a Principal who travels frequently to many locations, you may have no ability to complete any Site Advance field work. In these cases, efforts should be made to contact local site personnel in order to collect as much information as possible. If you cannot personally visit; are there maps, phone numbers or other data available that can be faxed or emailed? Are there local security officials that can accomplish some or all of the Site Advance field work?

Protection must be maintained at and between sites, and protection must be stable at and between sites.

- Collect relevant information during the Site Advance.
- Assign levels of risk to Targets.
- Once you assign risk levels, determine how it is you plan to keep those risks from rising above the acceptable level. Example: If you assigned a room a risk level of High, how will you reduce it to an acceptable level and *keep* it that way?
- Once a location is stabilized to an acceptable level, how will that level be maintained? Do you need Agents posted there? Do those areas need cameras with consistent monitoring?
- Along with specific Targets, these principles apply to routes and between sites as well.

Other things to consider while conducting Site Advance field work:

- What areas are public?
- What areas are available to the press?
- What areas are available to family and friends?
- What areas are available to security personnel?
- How are arrival and departure going to be secured?
- All of these questions should be answered. Once they are; how will you keep these areas from being contaminated or violated by people who are restricted from these areas?

## Filtering Risk

Peter M. Sandman is an expert in Risk Communications and suggests that Risk = hazard + outrage. Outrage and hazard do not carry equal weight. When hazard is high and outrage is low, people under-react based on their perception that everything is okay. When hazard is low and outrage is high, people over-react based on their perception things are horrible. Try to determine where the "real" risk is vs. perceived risk?

There is a filtering system for people and things that have proximity to the Asset or Principal. This system filters out risks from big to small. Physical, technological and psychological barriers can be used to eliminate or mitigate risks.

For example, you might assign a High Risk value to a room where the Principal will be meeting with other people. An example of using a physical barrier to reduce risk would be locking the access doors to the area where the room is located. An example of using a technological barrier to reduce risk would be to screen the people meeting with the Principal using metal detectors or to install cameras. An example of using a psychological barrier to reduce risk would be to assign an EP Agent to the meeting room.

As you conduct Site Advance field work on the identified Targets, you will be looking for vulnerabilities. Once you discover vulnerability, you should assign it a risk level. By doing so, you will be making it relatively easy to assign the resources you have available. Obviously, if you have limited resources you will be using them to deal with High risks as opposed to Low risks.

Since we already know that distance between the Principal and others is a significant factor in their safety, we can assign risk using distance as a barometer.

The Outer Perimeter
What is the outer perimeter of your Target area? Generally, with outer perimeter areas the rule is that there should be no obvious risk in these areas. These areas should be cleared of obvious risks and are generally assigned a low risk score. Your efforts are to discover obvious risks and remove them.

The Middle Perimeter
What is the middle perimeter of your Target area? Generally, with middle perimeter areas the rule is that there should be no hidden risk in these areas. These areas should be cleared of any hidden risks and are generally assigned a medium risk score. Your efforts are to discover and then secure areas in which it would be possible to hide risk – like a closet, or adjoining hallway or hidden compartments.

The Inner Perimeter
What is the inner perimeter of your Target area? Generally, with inner perimeter areas the rule is that there should be no ability for risk to enter – at all. These areas should be secured in such a manner that there is no possibility of risk entering the area. These areas are generally assigned a high risk score. Your efforts are to secure these areas in a manner that does not allow risk to enter. This requires screening and clearing an area – then constant monitoring of that area with screening procedures in place for anything that enters it.

One you determine risk scores (high, medium or low) it becomes very clear where resources need to be assigned. Example: If your Principal is the keynote speaker at a large event, the Ballroom may be swept before an event. But how will the visitors and attendees be observed and/or screened as they enter to insure no risk enters the Ballroom. Which areas will be under surveillance vs. just securing them? Who will have access to restricted areas?

We need to distinguish that although these are the goals - High, Medium and Low risk scores do not necessarily correspond to Outer, Middle and Inner Perimeters. Example: The place you park the vehicle might be in a parking lot, which technically is an Outer Perimeter. However, this is also a place where there should be no ability for risk to enter, particularly since we know that drop-off areas, pick-up areas and vehicles in general are common Targets for Adversaries. So, not everything in the Outer Perimeter is automatically assigned a Low Risk score. A ridiculous example might be a tank parked outside the building your VIP will be in – in a war-torn country. Although there may be a legitimate reason for it being there, you need to at least consider giving it a High risk score, depending on what you find out about the tank. Conversely, not everything assigned a Low Risk score is going to be found in the Outer perimeter. There will be Targets within the Inner Perimeter you will assign low risk scores to.

Beware. Filtering Risk can be taken to extremes. For example, you could assign the water that is provided to your Principal in a restaurant as a Target, because it could be tampered with or poisoned before it is given to him. That is a fact. However, if you look at the likely Methods of Operation you discovered while conducting Protective Intelligence your research should have indicated that there are not too many examples of VIP's being poisoned at events they are attending through the water they are given. So, although the poisoning of water is certainly a possibility, it is not likely. Most VIPs are attacked by a person, and in person. This should be your mindset when approaching your protection assignments. You cannot possibly protect someone from everything unless you have unlimited Agents and an unlimited budget at your disposal.

## Taking It To The Next Level

There are several things you can do to take this to the next level. My first suggestion is to go to a Mall as suggested at the end of Chapter 5. This would be the Mall that Mr. Santos will be giving a presentation at to promote his new book, followed by a meet and greet book signing and a Q&A with the Press. Find a main area in the Mall where it would make sense for this to take place. Then, look for Targets based on the principles presented in this chapter. Assign those Targets a risk score.

If you would like to stay much closer to home you can do this by simply designating an item in your home as the critical Asset. Then walk around the yard and the house looking for Targets. Or, pick a room in your house in which a VIP will be staying and do the same thing.

The point of either exercise is to get you to begin to look for, and evaluate Targets – those things which if degraded or destroyed put the Asset at risk – and assign those Targets risk scores based on the principles explained in this chapter. You do *not* have to figure out ways to eliminate or mitigate the risks you find; at least not yet. (That is coming in the next chapter.)

Create a prioritized list of your Targets. Once you have done this, begin to think about how you will address each Target in order to minimize the risks and vulnerabilities. This does not need to be exhaustive. Some readers will come up with long, creative lists of risks; helicopters landing on the roof and combatants bursting through the skylights. Creative - but unlikely at a book signing. You should be more interested in whether you can identify and prioritize realistic Targets. Just take your top 3 Targets and begin to work toward minimizing the risks they present. Your methods of minimizing risks will probably change as you continue to read through this book. In this exercise the focus should be on the principles of identifying and prioritizing Targets – *not* finding complete solutions for each one.

# 11
# VULNERABILITY ASSESSMENT OF TARGETS

The purpose of this chapter is to prime you for the things you should be considering while collecting and evaluating Target information and data. Targets are things, places, people, patterns, systems, etc. that, if destroyed, degraded or compromised, increase the vulnerability of the identified Asset.

At this point you have already identified Targets and assigned risk levels to them. This has helped you make decisions about allocating resources that you have available to you.

You need specific information before you can accurately calculate risk. There is a big difference between evaluating risk cognitively, which you have already done – and actually identifying specific vulnerabilities while considering solutions to mitigate the risk of those vulnerabilities. This requires Site Advance Field work. Example: Let's assume one of the identified critical Assets is a secret formula and we know one of the Targets for this formula is a locked room where the formula is kept. Let us also assume we have identified the primary threat (Adversary) to this critical Asset as a Criminal whose motivation is economic gain through the theft of this formula. We have conducted Protective Intelligence by studying and researching similar theft-of-formula-type cases along with theft and burglary tactics. We have also considered Insiders, which are often used in thefts of this type. We have identified the likely Method of Operation the Adversary will use to steal the formula. Now, in order to accurately calculate risk we need to actually see where this formula is kept.

When we assess vulnerabilities of Targets, we work from the outside in. The purpose of the assessment is to discover specific vulnerabilities and then initiate plans and systems that will effectively mitigate those risks – and close those vulnerabilities.

Consider several scenarios.

Scenario 1

As you drive up to the facility where the formula is kept, you notice a camera at the edge of the property. As you enter the parking lot you are met by a security guard who asks to see some type of identification then notes your license plate number and asks you to sign a Visitor Log. The guard gives you a numbered Visitor tag. You park and as you walk toward the front door, you notice cameras on the roof of the building. As you reach the front door you observe an alarm sign posted on the front door indicating the building has alarms and a monitoring system. You enter the building and are met by a receptionist who asks the purpose of your visit and who you would like to see. She asks you to wait while she calls the person you have identified, who comes to the reception desk to meet you. You are taken down a hallway to a locked door and you notice the door is armed with an alarm. You look up and observe another camera in the hallway. You ask about the camera and you are told that camera is monitored 24 hours a day, 7 days a week by a live person. The door is unlocked and you enter into a room that is alarmed with infrared beam sensor technology. The person escorting you turns to a pad on the wall and disarms the alarms using fingerprint technology. Your escort then leads you across the room to a heavy safe which they open by code. Inside the safe is a lockbox, which is where the formula is stored safely. How much risk is in this scenario?

Scenario 2

You drive up to the facility and park in the lot. You walk in the door and not seeing anyone around, begin to walk the hallways of the building looking for the person you are supposed to meet. After locating that person in an office, they take you to an unsecured room where they take a picture off the wall and reach into a hole in the wall. Out comes the formula in their hand. You express amazement and bewilderment. After all, this formula is an identified Asset that is critical to the success of the Mission. They tell you not to worry because only a few select people know about the location of the formula. How much risk is in this scenario?

The point of sharing these scenarios is to encourage you to visit and observe each Target location in order to accurately determine what risks need to be addressed. Determining the vulnerability of Targets usually requires Site Advance field work and observation. While assessing the vulnerability of these Targets you should be considering the following principles.

## Reducing Risk

There are three methods of approaching vulnerabilities and mitigating risk.

- Physical Barriers: These are defined as any type of physical barrier or object that becomes an obstacle for the Adversary. Examples would include fences, doors, burglar bars, gates, locks, etc.
- Technology: Defined as technological systems that provide barriers to the Adversary or surveillance of the Adversary.
- People: Defined as people who possess the requisite capabilities and training to respond appropriately to a threat, vulnerability or the Adversary's actions.

## Physical Barrier Primer & Checklist

The goal with Physical Barriers is to deter the Adversary. This is best accomplished by establishing barriers that all Adversaries perceive as too difficult to defeat. Deterrence, of course, is impossible to measure.

- Fencing: Fencing can be easily cut. In order for it to be an effective deterrent, the perception to the Adversary must be that it is a significant deterrent. Some types of fencing are fortified with barriers at the top or charged with electricity. Fencing should be well lit, with cameras monitoring those areas, or motion detection technology.
- Parking: If possible, parking should be restricted to 300 feet from the Target. If restricted parking is not feasible, properly identified vehicles should be parked closest to the Target and visitor vehicles parked at a distance. Keep the parking area and outside entrance doors clean and neat. Mount an obvious camera in the area. Keep "no parking" areas clear.
- Lighting: Surveys of criminals repeatedly show that lighting is a deterrent to criminal behavior.
- Shrubs and Vines: These should be kept close to the ground to reduce their potential to conceal the Adversary or their tools and weapons.
- Windows, Window boxes and Planters: These receptacles are perfect for the Adversary to hide tools and weapons. Unless there is an absolute requirement for such ornamentation, window boxes and planters are better removed. If they must remain, someone should be checking them regularly.

The ideal security situation is a building with no windows. However, bars, grates, heavy mesh screens, or steel shutters over windows offer good protection from otherwise unwanted entry. It is important that the openings in the protective coverings are not too large. Otherwise, a weapon (explosive or other) may be introduced into the building while the Adversary remains outside. Floor vents, transoms, and skylights should also be covered. Fire safety considerations preclude the use of certain window coverings. Municipal ordinances should be researched and safety considered before any of these renovations are undertaken.

- Entrance & Exit Doors: Ideally, these doors will have hinges and hinge pins on the inside to prevent removal from the outside. Solid wood or sheet metal faced doors provide extra integrity that a hollow-core wooden door cannot provide. A steel door frame that properly fits the door is as important as the construction of the door. Locks should be keyed and have the bump-proof Grade 1 ANSI designation deadbolt type.
- Controlled Access: Controlled access is the easiest method of controlling an Adversary's ability to access certain areas. Controlled access starts at the outer perimeter of the Target and considers all close proximity movements as well. Controls should be established for positively identifying those who have authorized access to Target areas and for denying access to unauthorized people. These controls should extend to the inspection of all packages and materials being taken into Target areas.

If the Target is a building, Security and Maintenance personnel should be alert for people who act in a suspicious manner, as well as objects, items, or parcels which look out of place or suspicious. Regular checks should be established to include potential hiding places – like stairwells, rest rooms, and any vacant office spaces - for unwanted individuals. Doors or access ways to such areas as boiler rooms, mail rooms, computer areas, switchboards, and elevator control rooms should remain locked when not in use. It is important to establish a procedure for the accountability of keys. If keys cannot be accounted for, locks should be changed.

If the Target is a building, perhaps entrances and exits can be modified with a minimal cost to channel all visitors through someone at a main reception desk. Individuals entering the building would be required to sign a register indicating the name and room number of the person with whom they wish to visit. Employees at these reception desks could contact the person to be visited and advise him/her that a visitor, by name, is in the lobby. The person to be visited may decide to come to the lobby to ascertain that the purpose of the visit is valid. A system for signing out when the visitor departs could be integrated into this procedure. Such a procedure might result in complaints from the public. If the reception desk employee explains to the visitor that these procedures were implemented in the best interest of safety, the complaints will be reduced. The placement of a sign at the reception desk informing visitors of the need for safety is another option.

- Housekeeping: Good housekeeping is also vital. Trash or dumpster areas should remain free of debris. A tool or weapon can easily be concealed in the trash. Combustible materials should be properly disposed of or protected if further use is anticipated.

## Technology Primer & Checklist
The goal with Technology is to detect and deter the Adversary. This is best accomplished by establishing technology that all Adversaries perceive as too difficult to defeat. Deterrence, of course, can be difficult to measure.

- Cameras: For covert surveillance it is preferable to have the camera camouflaged, as most internal cameras are. We use these cameras to catch the Adversary doing something wrong, but do not want them to know they are being watched. Most people do not look up, in any situation, unless prompted to do so. That is why these cameras work well in those situations. However, for deterrence, you want the Adversary to know there is a camera watching them. The camera does not have to be real but it should be obvious. After all, perception is most people's reality. Camera surveillance is an option for potential hiding places such as stairwells, rest rooms, and any vacant office spaces in order to detect unwanted individuals.
- Alarms: If the Target is a building there should be an adequate burglar alarm system installed by a reputable company that can service and properly maintain the equipment. Post signs indicating that such a system is in place.
- Detection Devices: Install detection devices at all entrances and closed-circuit television in those areas previously identified as likely places where an Adversary might place a tool or weapon. This, coupled with the posting of signs indicating such measures are in place, is a good deterrent.

## People Primer & Checklist
The goal with People is to enlist qualified personnel who possess the requisite capabilities and training to respond appropriately to an Adversary's actions. This is best accomplished by establishing excellent recruitment methods and appropriate training.

- Highly Visible Security Patrol & Plainclothes Personnel: Research suggests that plainclothes store detectives have only a limited impact on shoplifting. A study in a large London music store showed the store would need to hire 17 times more than the 4 store detectives they had on duty to catch all the shoplifters likely to enter the store. How does this apply to you? Advertising a uniformed officer's presence has a greater deterrent effect than a plainclothes officer but it may also mean that shoplifters exercise greater caution. Little is known from research about the effectiveness of the uniformed security guard. In general, guards who continually move around and create an active, visible presence are likely to be more effective.

This research is applicable to the decision-making process of whether to use security personnel for a protection detail and how they are deployed.

Consider matching a uniform officer with a plainclothes Agent for every hour of security coverage. They provide two very distinct functions. My anecdotal research indicates this is the best combination to deter criminal behavior. One without the other simply lacks the overall effectiveness they have working together. If the budget allows only one officer, I recommend an officer in uniform who spends a great deal of their time concentrating on the identified Target areas. A highly visible security patrol can be a significant deterrent. Even if this "patrol" is only one security guard, they could be optimally utilized outside the building. If an interior guard is utilized, consider the installation of closed circuit television cameras that cover exterior building perimeters.

Instruct all security personnel to make direct eye contact and speak to as many people as possible. Public relations are one of the easiest and most effective ways of deterring criminal behavior. Most Adversaries want privacy. Great public relations reduce the Adversary's privacy through visible contact and direct communication. This direct communication translates into an unconscious message of "bonding" between the officer and the potential Adversary. It unconsciously deters the notion of criminal behavior. Depending on the type of Adversary, it may be more difficult for them to harm someone they think they know, rather than a complete stranger. Make people feel welcome. Make them feel happy. Make them feel that you are ready to help them with their needs. Start a conversation; anything to create a bond.

In the event that a security officer suspects a person is an Adversary, the officer should immediately approach them and initiate contact while observing behavioral clues. The Adversary may think the officer has just observed them doing something that has given away their intentions. If the Adversary's perception is that they have become suspicious to security personnel, they are likely leave the area as quickly as possible. There are several ways of handling this. The security person can allow the Adversary to leave. If security personnel are certain the Adversary has initiated some criminal behavior, they may intervene.

Properly selected and appropriately trained security personnel are invaluable in the detection and observation of inappropriate or unusual human behavior, which are hallmark indicators of adversarial intentions. However, they need to be trained in what to look for.

## Final Note to this Chapter

It is highly unlikely that you will have the luxury of conducting a Site Advance as thoroughly as this chapter suggests, unless;

- You have been retained to plan security far in advance of an event.
- You are working on a large team.
- You are working for someone whose itinerary is known well ahead of time and can afford to send you out ahead of time to do this type of advance work.

The reality is that you may have to apply these principles rapidly while spontaneously assessing Targets and their vulnerabilities; assigning them risk scores while simultaneously making rushed decisions about applying Physical, Technological or People solutions to mitigate risks – and, you may have to accept more risk than you would like to.

One other thing. You do *not* have to actually apply the Physical Barriers, Technology or People Solutions at this stage of preparation and planning. Some of them may carry a cost to implement. You may not have the authority to authorize these types of expenses. You should, however, be prepared to present your findings to those decision-makers who have that authority.

Your primary task at this point is to put together a coherent plan that is worthy of a professional presentation.

## Taking It To The Next Level

This one is pretty simple. Just look at the Targets you discovered at the end of the last Chapter. Then, look at the Physical Barrier, Technology and People sections of this chapter and begin to apply solutions to the vulnerabilities. Your goal, of course, is to reduce the risk scores of each Target vulnerability.

# 12
# GENERAL EMERGENCY PLANNING

You could experience an actual emergency during a protection detail that you might need to respond to. These types of emergencies are not necessarily attacks directed toward your Principal, but they are events which could jeopardize the safety of your Principal or Asset.

For example, there could be a real fire at a store in the Mall that has nothing to do with Mr. Santos – except for the fact he happens to be there. If something like this were to happen you are still responsible for his safety. As a protection Agent, don't get locked into a mind-set that would exclude real emergencies in your planning.

Here is a quick overview of some emergencies that could happen, along with some tips. You do not need specific contingency plans for every conceivable emergency but you should do some general emergency planning.

<u>Bomb</u>
- What were the characteristics of the threat? (call time, place, gender, caller ID) Did the threat contain specific location information? People who give specific information have a tendency to be more truthful than those who speak in broad generalities.
- Does a search need to be conducted? Turn this function over to augmented security or law enforcement. If you do conduct a search, use a grid pattern to insure you covered everything.
- Do you need to evacuate? If so, to where, and how will you get there?
- Do you know where the exits are?
- If you find a suspicious package, turn the disposal function over to augmented security or law enforcement.

Power Failure
- Do you need to evacuate? If so, to where, and how will you get there?
- Do you know where the exits are?
- If possible, augmented security should be used to investigate rather than sacrificing Agent coverage of the Principal.
- Do you carry a flashlight?

Fire
- Do you need to evacuate? If so, to where, and how will you get there?
- Do you know where the exits are?
- If possible, augmented security should be used to investigate rather than sacrificing Agent coverage of the Principal.

Civil Disturbance
- Are you aware of the political climate, crime rates and demographics of the area you are in? This should be part of your Protective Intelligence.
- Do you need to evacuate? If so, to where, and how will you get there?
- Do you know where the exits are?
- If possible, augmented security should be used to investigate rather than sacrificing Agent coverage of the Principal.

Robbery
- Have you established secure areas or a safe room?
- Isolate the Principal from the threat.
- Do you need to evacuate? If so, to where, and how will you get there?
- Do you know where the exits are?
- If possible, augmented security should be used to investigate rather than sacrificing Agent coverage of the Principal.
- If need be, neutralize and capture the Adversary.

Hostage
- Have you established secure areas or a safe room?
- Isolate the Principal from the threat.
- Do you need to evacuate? If so, to where, and how will you get there?

- Do you know where the exits are?
- Isolate the threat and secure perimeters.
- Stabilize the situation.
- If possible, augmented security should be used to investigate rather than sacrificing Agent coverage of the Principal.
- If need be, negotiate.

Assault

- Have you established secure areas or a safe room?
- Isolate the Principal from the threat.
- Do you need to evacuate? If so, to where, and how will you get there?
- Do you know where the exits are?
- Isolate the threat and secure perimeters.
- Stabilize the situation.
- If possible, augmented security should be used to investigate rather than sacrificing Agent coverage of the Principal.
- If need be, neutralize and capture the Adversary.

Medical Emergency

- If possible, augmented security and EMS personnel should be used to handle medical emergencies.
- Sometimes medical emergencies can be chaotic, depending on the size and scope of the emergency.
- Have you established secure areas or a safe room?
- Do you need to evacuate? If so, to where, and how will you get there?
- Do you know where the exits are?

If you work with a large team of Agents there should be one designated Commander for all types of emergencies. Agents should be trained in multiple response capabilities. It would be prudent to have an emergency checklist available. These can be printed and laminated and given to Agents. It may be difficult to determine if the emergency is an actual emergency or a diversion. You must treat them all seriously.

## Taking It To The Next Level

There is good research that strongly suggests we can program our brains to respond with excellence through visualization. The brain operates like a computer search engine. It looks for solutions when we enter a situation that requires a response. If there is no "data" entered into your brain, no solution is found. Think about it. If no one has ever taught you how to change a flat tire you will have little success trying to do this when it happens. However, if you have ever changed a tire, or read about how to – that is where your brain goes to find the solution.

In one of the most well-known studies on Creative Visualization in sports, Russian scientists compared four groups of Olympic athletes in terms of their training schedules:

- Group 1 had 100% physical training;
- Group 2 had 75% physical training with 25% mental training;
- Group 3 had 50% physical training with 50% mental training;
- Group 4 had 25% physical training with 75% mental training.
- Group 4, with 75% of their time devoted to mental training, performed the best. The Soviets figured out that we can affect outcomes through mental training.

Taking this chapter's principles to the next level is very simple. Look at the list of emergencies and visualize these happening, one at a time, to either Mr. Santos at the Mall – or to your designated Asset in your home.

How will you respond to each one? Is there anything you can do in the planning stages or the site advance work to prepare for these emergencies?

# 13
# GATHERING POLICY & PROCEDURES

What policies and procedures are already in place that will mitigate or increase risk to the Assets? These questions should be answered in the context of each identified Target. If possible, copies of policies and procedures should be obtained.

You may find that simply creating a policy or updating an existing procedure may reduce a risk. For example, if all the external doors to a building are open during weekly business hours at your location, anyone can walk in. If all the doors were secured during business hours except the main entrance, and just inside the main entrance a visitor is met by the receptionist, risk has been significantly reduced. This is a perfect example of how policies and procedures affect risks.

Another example would be to have EMS personnel on stand-by at the Mall for the Mr. Santos speaking event and book signing. By doing so you have eliminated a lot of risk in the event of a medical emergency. Now, if you added some police and fire and security personnel as well, and you positioned them properly – giving them the specific roles of looking for and attending to any General Emergencies - you have effectively reduced the consequences of a General Emergency because you have people in place that are proactively looking for these situations to develop and will respond immediately. You discover this works so well that you decide this should be policy anytime Mr. Santos appears in a large, public setting.

Get it?

If you are an EP Agent your ability to influence policies and procedures can range from almost nothing - to great ability. In the case of Mr. Santos, for instance, you will ultimately have to deal with the airport security procedures and mall security procedures. They may have policies in place that are not to your liking. You should always discuss your concerns with decision-makers who have the ability to change or modify policies and procedures which will affect the safety of your Asset.

Sometimes, you will find policies in place that will enhance your ability to protect your Asset. Another example: Some malls in the United States have police officers that are brought in routinely to work large events. This would be a bonus for you. It gives you some extra bodies, eyes and ears. You would also, presumably, have some influence on where these officers are positioned and what they are assigned to do – particularly if you are planning the security for that event.

The simplest way to figure this out is to think of the places and buildings your Asset will be in. Then, determine a contact person for each organization, building or entity you will be encountering. These "contacts" are people you should be speaking to as part of your advance planning. From them, you will be learning *their* procedure and policy information that will potentially affect the safety of your Asset.

If I were to cut to the core of this principle with something easily understood by most people, consider this. Fire doubles in size about every 30-60 seconds. If, by policy, you have fire extinguishers located throughout a building and employees know where they are located and how to use them, you have greatly reduced the amount of risk that comes from fire. Apply this type of thinking toward your Asset. When conducting Site Advance work, check to see what procedures and policies are in place that will reduce risk. It will help you decide how to allocate resources.

### Common Questions To Ask

Developing questions about policy and procedures will not be applicable to every Target. For instance, the vehicle that your Asset is transported in may have been identified as a Target by definition; because the Asset will be in it at some point. But the vehicle itself does not have policies and procedures that can be changed to enhance the safety of your Asset. You can rent an armored vehicle. You, as the driver, can change speed, routes and driving tactics – but there is no contact person to speak with about the policies of the vehicle. So, even though you would be referring to your prioritized Target list to identify what policies and procedures you need to know about – not every Target is going to have policies and procedures available.

Here are some questions that you might consider asking others that you have professional contact with about protecting your Asset. These questions do not necessarily need to be answered for every Target. Rather, they are included in this chapter with the intent of moving your thinking into the proper context. If you were assigned a permanent detail, such as protecting a business or a CEO in a full-time capacity – you would want permanent resolution to the issues that these questions raise.

- Are there any operational or security policies & procedures in place and implemented which will serve to mitigate or increase risk?
- Are those policies available to all staff? Has staff been trained in these procedures?
- Are there occurrence reporting procedures and documentation in place and implemented? This allows you to look back over time and identify common problems that need to be addressed.
- If there are no occurrence reporting procedures and documentation in place, what records are kept, and what is the minimum access time for retrieval of those records?
- Are operational staff and other on-site personnel aware of and trained in policies, procedures and occurrence reporting procedures?
- If there are operational staff present, does recurrent training happen at scheduled intervals?

These questions do not need to be answered for every Target. If anything, they are included in this chapter to encourage you to think about these things. More commonly, these questions should be answered if you are in a consulting role or your full-time position is acting in a security capacity for a business or person. These questions are less applicable for a one-time protection event or detail. They should, however, cause you to think about how policies and procedures can enhance or detract from your ability to provide protection.

## Taking It To The Next Level

If you are using your home-based designated Asset as a reference point, think of policies and procedures you could put into place for each Target you found – that might enhance the safety of the Asset.

If you are using a Mall as your reference point, make a list of the agencies, organizations or people you would want to talk to and what you would want to find out from them in terms of policies and procedures.

# 14
# PRINCIPLES FOR PRINCIPALS

There is another scenario worth considering and that is the situation in which you are not necessarily providing protection for a specific person. "Protection" and "Security" are broad terms that cover everything from planning for an event to providing general building security to escorting cash from point A to point B. Remember that the themes and principles you are reading about can be used to evaluate just about any type of risk; it just depends on where you apply the principles.

Regardless, at this point if you have followed the chronological order of this book, you have:

- Defined the Mission.
- Identified the critical Assets.
- Conducted an Asset Survey.
- Identified the Primary Threat or Adversary.
- Identified the Likely Method of Operation.
- Conducted Protective Intelligence.
- Identified Targets and Target Vulnerabilities.
- Applied Solutions to those Vulnerabilities through Physical Barriers, Technology or People.
- Planned for General Emergencies.
- Gathered and analyzed applicable Policies & Procedures.
- Put together a simple and coherent plan to present to decision-makers regarding your findings and assessment.

## The Chat

Several years ago I conducted an extensive simulation at the end of a year-long training effort with a group of EP Agents that were assigned a wealthy husband-wife team as Principals. I recruited outside actors as role players, including the person who would play the "Principal" during this simulation. This simulation lasted about 5 hours and started when they picked up the Principal at a private airport. It ended back at the airport after several appointments the Principal was to be transported to, including private meetings and supper at a restaurant. This team of Agents were given several months to plan for this simulation. I recruited multiple role-players that would present various issues to these Agents during the simulation. The Agents had planned this evening so well and had acted so professionally that people in the restaurant were asking who the person playing the role of the Principal was. Restaurant staff were asking the Agents what was going on. Local police kept driving by trying to figure out why there were people with wires in their ears standing outside of a restaurant on this warm summer evening.

The night went along smoothly and the problems my role-players were throwing at these Agents were being handled impressively. As an instructor who has spent this much time with a group of trainees, this is exactly what you hope to see. I decided to change things up. Acting as the Principal's executive assistant during the simulation so I could observe it in great detail, I privately asked the Principal to tell the Agents that he was uncomfortable with them invading his "space-bubble", which for most people is about 2 arm's-length distance. Up to that point in the evening they had positioned themselves to be within 2 arm's-length distance of the Principal or within 2 arm's-length distance of anyone who approached the Principal. Now, the Principal was telling these Agents to back off and give him space. He was also acting a bit cranky and irritated. This threw the Agents off of their game. They acted intimidated and almost apologetic. By the time we got back to the airport to put the Principal back on the plane, the team of Agents was in a bit of disarray. Through a ruse one of the role players attacked the Principal with a knife, which several EP Agents successfully dealt with – but in the process the Principal's face was smashed against a wall because of positioning even though I successfully intervened to cushion the blow.

The point? You can't always get what you want. These Agents wanted to position themselves within 2 arm's-length distance of the Principal and anyone who approached the Principal, which worked well until the Principal changed the rules. At that point these Agents could not get what they wanted or get what they thought they needed from the Principal to keep him safe.

How do you get those things that you want so that you can effectively protect the Principal? You have to have "the chat". Or, you have someone else have "the chat" on your behalf; the VIP's administrative assistant, the road manager or someone else who has the authority to do it. What does the "chat" consist of? Basically, it is a briefing in which the Principal is informed about the following Principles.

Before we begin to explore these things together, let me share one other quick story. A friend of mine is in the protection business and owns a protection company. Recently, he provided protection for a Celebrity at an event. In preparation for this he requested an Asset Survey (see chapter 6) from the Celebrity. He went through the proper channels. Soon after, he received a phone call from this VIP's manager who, in heated and somewhat vulgar terms accused my friend of being unprofessional because of the Asset Survey request.

Really? If they could not provide some simple answers that would enhance the safety of the Celebrity then why did they hire anyone to do the protection?

**Principles for Principals**
If you can pull this off with the Principal, several things get accomplished. The first one is that they know that you know what you are doing, because what you are doing is based on solid research. The second thing you accomplish is to shift some of the burden of protection on them by virtue of their cooperation with the plan you have put together.

Here is what every Principal should know, based on solid research and statistical probabilities.
- Since most attacks are over within 5 seconds the EP Agent needs to position themselves appropriately because when they are properly positioned they almost always prevail when an attack occurs.
- Safety is greatly enhanced when there is a minimum of 25 feet between the Principal and the public.
- Avoid any delays around or near the vehicle.
- Secrecy: Any time a member of the public can discover where the Principal will be – risk rises.
- Although most people are not interested in the presence, movements and behavior of the EP Agent – the Adversary is keenly interested. Perception is everything to the Adversary. Every public appearance allows the professional perception of the EP Agent to dissuade the Adversary's intent.

- To whatever extent is possible, always arrive and depart using non-public routes and areas.

Principals who grant EP Agents great discretion in security arrangements and listen to the EP Agent's intuition – and do *not* give the EP Agent menial tasks and responsibilities, greatly enhance their own safety.

## Specifying Undesirable Consequences

Providing Undesirable Consequences to decision-makers may have an impact on getting what you need. Now that you have a plan put together, you need it authorized to begin to implement it.

The reality is that most Executive Protection Agents work alone or as part of a small detail and as such, there may be a lot of risk you just have to accept. Obviously, the higher risk Targets with great vulnerabilities are those which you want to take care of first. Let's add another factor. Consider the Undesirable Consequences of Targets being attacked. It is very difficult to protect all the identified Assets all the time, or to protect an identified Asset from all possible risks. Therefore, you need to make decisions as to what risks are acceptable. This process of Specifying Undesirable Consequences will help you further choose how to manage your resources.

Look at your list of prioritized Targets. Each Target should have a Low, Medium or High risk value given to it. Remember that Low risk means "no apparent risk can enter". Medium risk means "no hidden risk can enter". High risk means "no risk can enter". Consider the following questions.

- What are the most valuable Targets?
- Which identified Targets, if destroyed, degraded or compromised; open up the greatest vulnerabilities to the identified Assets? These would most likely be the Targets you have assigned as High risk.
- What is the economic loss if an attack is successful at one of the Targets?
- What is the probable loss of life if an attack is successful at one of the Targets?
- What is the loss of Mission if an attack is successful at one of the Targets?

Why are these questions important?

In the case of Mr. Tommy Santos, he is speaking at a Mall. You have been retained to protect him. If an Adversary detonates an Improvised Explosive Device (IED) in the middle of the Mall, will the loss of life be acceptable?

Will the economic loss to the Mall be acceptable? You may be thinking: "My job is to protect Mr. Santos, not everyone else in the Mall." That may be true. But if suicide bombers successfully detonate IED's at two consecutive speaking engagements of Mr. Santos, he will not be speaking publicly again for a long time. If he did, people would not come to see him out of fear. You will also carry the reputation that on your watch, an IED was detonated at a Mall event potentially causing many deaths and thousands of dollars in damage.

So, the answers to these questions become important and they encourage the decision-makers (or your Principal) to look at things differently. The Mall and its occupants may not be your problem. The only way you will know that is if you consider these questions. If you were worried about a suicide bomber in regards to Mr. Santos you will probably be working in close conjunction with mall security and local police to mitigate the risk of suicide bombers – even though a suicide bomber may not be the indentified Adversary or the Primary Threat.

Let me be clear. I am not suggesting that you need to consider suicide bombers as part of your protection planning with Mr. Santos. In fact, I am using suicide bombers in this example because they are an unlikely risk at an event like this. The point here is that you need to consider Undesirable Consequences of a successful attack against one of your Targets. That attack may not necessarily put your Principal at risk but it might put others at risk and it may create an enormous economic loss that has far-reaching consequences. This may not be your primary responsibility but it is something you need to consider in planning.

## Taking It To The Next Level

Using either your home-based scenario or the Santos event, answer the following questions.

- What are the most valuable Targets?
- Which identified Targets, if destroyed, degraded or compromised; open up the greatest vulnerabilities to the identified Assets? These would most likely be the Targets you have assigned as High risk.
- What is the economic loss if an attack is successful at one of the Targets?
- What is the probable loss of life if an attack is successful at one of the Targets?
- What is the loss of Mission if an attack is successful at one of the Targets?

# 15
# POST OPERATIONS

Now that your plan of protection has been authorized it is time to implement it. Preferably, much of the implementation is delegated. I am a big fan of delegation. Just make sure the people you delegate the tasks to are people that are competent in what you are asking them to do. If you are a one-person or small-person detail that is working while you are on the move, you must adapt and do the best you can using the principles within this book as a foundation.

## Command Post Operations

A Command Post or Command Center is the communications center. Usually these are used with large teams, large events or high-risk VIPs. You may never see one if you work alone or you are part of a small detail.

Command Post Operations consist of receiving, collecting, analyzing and recording all information, then prioritizing that information into useful instructions for Agents in Post positions.

In very large operations there may be two command posts; a Protection Detail Command Post and a General Security Command Post. Each one handles exactly what their names suggest. If you have the luxury of having both, they should be located in close proximity to each other so they can work together in determining what actions should be taken with any incoming information.

Again, if you work alone or with a small detail you will rarely see a Command Post, much less have the ability to establish one.

## Post Operations

Post operations are the expectations and responsibilities that are carried out at each position that an Agent is placed, or posted. The number of Posts that you use is almost entirely dependent on the number of Agents available for the detail.

From a practical standpoint, you should assign Posts in a method that will detect risks and potential problems from as many angles and as far away from potential problems as possible; DIG. This makes Post placement critical. In order to detect and discover problems, you need to be able to be in a position to do so. Agents at any Post should be practicing DIG; looking for unusual and inappropriate behavior. Once detected, some type of evaluation and/or investigation should take place.

Things that are discovered as part of DIG cannot be ignored. They cannot be shelved. They must be decided upon so that the Agent can stay in the moment looking for the next potential problem. This does not mean that an EP Agent who uncovers something needs to leave their Post to go investigate further but they should have the discretion to do so if necessary. Obviously, communicating to other Agents those things which are uncovered during DIG is important. Alternatives to leaving a Post position is to have a proxy (someone else) investigate the discovered concern. Other tips for assigning Post positions include:

- Assign and list Posts by priority when you plan.
- Post placements should be in view of each other to the extent that is practical.
- Low visibility of the Agent is a goal on each Post position.
- If you expect a long duration on a particular Post be prepared to leap frog (rotate) the Posts. Keep in mind, however, that any critical information or surveillance must be passed during the rotation between Agents. Example: The Agent at the X Post has been observing a suspicious person with inappropriate behavior. This information needs to be passed on to the new Agent posting at the X Post.
- A jump team or primary Agent always stays with the Asset/Principal from site to site.

## Taking It To The Next Level

Taking the next logical step and using either your home-based scenario or the Tommy Santos event at the Mall:

- Assign Post positions. Keep in mind as you do this what your most vulnerable Targets are.
- Create Post responsibilities and expectations. These are commonly referred to as Post Orders.
- Assign a location for the Command Post.

It stands to reason that your top Targets will have Agents posted at them, but this is not always the case. For instance, while you were planning you may have originally discovered vulnerability within a Target that you assigned "risk cannot enter", which would be a High risk score. If this was an open hallway and you locked the doors to it along with placing camera surveillance at that location, you have effectively reduced risk to an acceptable level, thereby eliminating the need for an Agent to be posted there. However, you may feel that even with the doors locked and camera surveillance you still need to assign an Agent to a Post position there. This is entirely dependent on circumstances. As you can see, part of this planning is subjective to your perception and determination of risk.

For this particular exercise you are looking to sharpen your ability to assign Post positions and create Post orders. Try to create 5 Post positions and indicate where they are located, along with Post orders for each of those positions.

If you are actually visiting your local Mall as you read through this book, there are restricted areas in Malls that you will not be able to enter. You may decide to locate the Command Center in one of these restricted areas. Command Centers do not always need to be hidden. Instead, they need to be efficient. Also, many malls in the United States added extensive camera surveillance and Homeland Security cameras in the post 9/11 age of Terrorism. As such, you may be approached by Mall Security while conducting some of the Site Advance work suggested in this book. I encourage you to be forthright and respectful should you be approached by security or law enforcement personnel. The field work suggested in this book does not violate any statutes or ordinances. However, your behavior at a Mall could trigger an approach by security personnel.

# 16
# FOREIGN TRAVEL & KIDNAPPING

Several things will affect your approach to protection when traveling internationally. The internet and free trade agreements have given us a global economy. This has increased international travel for many business people. Post 9/11, there has been a tremendous increase in terror related kidnappings and violence against foreigners. Some of this stems from simple opportunism by gangs and criminals to make some money. Some of it is driven by ideology.

The reasons are, to some degree, irrelevant if you are an EP Agent. It is unlikely that you will have any ability to affect the motivation or goals of these people. If there is any value in understanding the motivation and goals of those who purposely commit violence against foreigners or are interested in kidnapping your Principal, it is to adopt strategies that keep your Principal off of their radar.

Kidnappers are not unlike other criminals. Some are sloppy and some are highly organized terrorists motivated by political goals or financial gain. Some use extensive planning and research to target victims while "express" kidnappings are generally short-lived with a goal of getting the victim to extract money from a nearby ATM machine. For the most part, money is the goal. The data on kidnapping varies dramatically.

One company that provides kidnap insurance reports the average ransom paid in 67% of the cases they insure is $2 million. Another source reports in one year the average amount paid in reported kidnap for ransom cases was $62,000 and that the many unreported cases of kidnap abroad pay as little as few hundred dollars.

## Kidnapping Facts

According to Insurance Carrier AIG's Crisis Management Division in Philadelphia, 48% of kidnap for ransom incidents occur in Latin America. 80% of kidnap for ransom cases are left unreported. Many sources report that less than 20% of kidnap cases are reported. Several sources suggest the actual number of kidnap cases is 5 times greater then what is reported. Why? Many people who receive ransom demands do not trust authorities to successfully deal with it in a professional manner. In many cases, law enforcement officials may have some implicit involvement in the incident and in some countries are directly involved.

It is easy to think about kidnappings as an almost exclusively foreign event carried out by terrorists, rebel armies and criminals. However, there are Executive kidnappings that occur in the United States. Bank branch managers and their families are at particular risk. Each year the FBI investigates 350 to 400 domestic kidnappings with ransom involved in one-third of the cases. Studies indicate that Americans with kidnap insurance fair 4 times better than their uninsured counterparts. This is because good insurance companies who specialize in kidnap insurance also bring serious experience and resources to the table in resolving kidnap cases.

According to Gavin De Becker's research, which I think is more accurate than many sources:

- The FBI reports 500-600 kidnap investigations per year. Many of these cases turn out not to be kidnappings. It is a large problem in other nations. In 2006 there were 15,000 incident worldwide.
- Leftist guerillas and rebels are primarily responsible.
- One study reports 66% of hostages are released, 20% are rescued, 9% are killed and 5% escape.

Regardless, the bottom line for you is three-fold:

- Plan appropriately.
- Keep your Principal/Asset in a low-profile mode.
- Train to react properly in an emergency.

## Understanding the Beast

Most kidnappings occur at the place of residence (or hotel) and on travel routes. This is fairly consistent with normal Executive Protection concerns, in which most attacks occur at arrival and departure areas. Solution: Instruct the Principal to vary the times of travel and the routes of travel anywhere while in the country. Consider switching hotels every day or two.

Most kidnappers are "insiders". The kidnapper profile is a physically fit male who is often well-educated, non-conspicuous, a member of the indigenous population with a former military or security background and is familiar with weapons use, self defense, tactics & explosives. They are highly motivated, either by political cause or money, and have carried out significant planning in terms of intelligence gathering, preparation and rehearsal. They carry out tasks with very little empathy or sensitivity but a high degree of emotional self-control. Solution: Trust no one. Limit contact with locals to those only required. Know your Principal's weaknesses and vulnerabilities. Employ counter-surveillance tactics. Train to deal with emergencies. Have multiple escape routes for every location.

Many kidnappers are well equipped. They use disguises as needed. They forge documents if required. They have all the tools they need, including weapons, to carry out their task. At the point of attack a drug is often immediately administered to the victim. Any and all types of transportation are used. Solution: Can the Principal perform the required tasks electronically from afar, without physically visiting the foreign country?

Overwhelmingly, the greatest obstacle that kidnap groups face if funding. All of the actions they take require significant funding. Because most of these groups prefer to remain low profile, their primary method of pre-kidnap surveillance is following the Principal's movements through fixed or moving surveillance. Solution: Look around and see who is following you, or who seems to be consistently in the same spot – which is in view of the Principal's locations.

In the world of violent crime the goal is to make the potential victim a "lousy and poor" victim. This encourages the Adversary to move on to someone else; a "good" victim. If you know what a kidnapper does and what they need to be successful, and you take those things away – they move on to someone else. The kidnapper's perception of their ability to be successful also has great bearing on their motivation. This comes down to two things.

How many things that the kidnapper needs to be successful, can you remove? How can you affect the kidnapper's perception of their ability to succeed?

Using the information above, how much risk do you remove by doing these things?

- Have the Principal conduct business electronically from different locations.
- Keep the Principal "low-profile" in terms of visibility.
- Remove any predictability of residence, travel routes and schedules.

- Interact with as few "locals", or strangers, as possible.
- Always complete appropriate planning and training for emergencies.
- Discover multiple escape routes and "safe" rooms or zones.
- Use counter-surveillance.
- Use the element of surprise to your benefit. Your Principal's movements should be a constant surprise to the Adversary.

## How to Conduct Surveillance and Counter-Surveillance

These activities allow you to identify others who are monitoring the activities of your Principal or Asset. The Adversary may have you or the Principal under surveillance. You must make attempts to detect whether this is taking place. Your goal is to monitor those people who are watching the Principal.

### Methods used in Surveillance

- Fixed from a fixed point. This is usually accomplished by people, but not necessarily.
- Moving on foot or vehicle. This is usually accomplished by people, but not necessarily.
- Technical: Using equipment. This might include cameras or listening devices.

### Counter Surveillance Methods

- Identify as many of the Principal's routes and locations as possible.
- Detect, limit and evaluate any choke points and other ideal attack sites or potentially dangerous sites.
- Locate medical facilities and safe relocation sites.
- Statistically, residence and work place routes are the most dangerous.

If you put yourself into the mind and shoes of the person watching you, just look around from every vantage point adjacent to your Principal.

## Before a Trip Abroad

- Check State Department Travel warnings.
- Know the location and phone number of the nearest US embassy, but make sure it is the number for its 24-hour security office and regional security officer. Carry a cell phone with appropriate emergency numbers placed in speed dial. Make sure your cell phone has international coverage.
- Consider appropriate vaccinations and bring sanitizer. One drop of bleach in 8 ounces of water makes it potable. Do you need to bring anti-virals?

- What plan is in place that will cover hospital treatment or medical evacuation? Does the insurance policy cover this?
- Have you given any thought to emergency exit plans from the country?
- Passports should be current. Make copies and have a supply of visa photos.
- Itinerary: Resolve conflicts ASAP and distribute the itinerary on a "need to know" only basis.
- Equipment: As needed and required.
- Personal luggage: Check to insure there are no restricted items or articles.
- Reconfirm auxiliary protection support you may need in country.
- Develop working relationships with Embassy and host country officials.
- Will there be any language translation issues?
- Are you aware of country protocol and cultural customs?

## In Country

- Technical and Document Security: Do you need secure voice and fax?
- Will you conduct routine IED sweeps?
- Is the luggage secure?
- Beware of others watching you or the Principal and conduct counter-surveillance.
- Wealth is relative, and anyone can be kidnapped. Middle class Americans are rich from a global view. As such, maintain a low profile with jewelry, clothing and transportation. Consider carrying a dummy wallet with small bills and old credit cards; keeping the real one hidden.
- Downplay your nationality. Try to dress like locals.
- Keep your passport safe.
- Vary all routines.
- Be wary of taxis. Use only official taxis.
- Stay away from isolated and rural areas. Travel on well-lit and well-traveled roads.
- Travel in groups. Two people present reduce the risk of violence by 80+%. Three people present; up to 95%.
- Petty crime is probably still the #1 risk. Lock valuables in the hotel safe. Carry minimal cash and a copy of your ID. Consider carrying a flash drive with critical documents. In the event of a kidnapping you

will either have them handy as a resource or be able to easily discard it if the information is not something you would want your captors to have access to. Consider leaving the laptop or iPad at home.

- Know where you are going. Looking at maps or asking for directions is an encouraging sign to criminals.
- Wash hands obsessively and drink bottled water only.
- During transports, have the Principal sit in the front passenger seat. He will look less important.
- In the unlikely event of a military coup, know where Western hotels are and how to get to one. Keep some extra $ and cheap bribes handy in case the food supply runs short or you need to catch a ride once the airport reopens.

## If You Are Kidnapped
- Know the facts. Most kidnap victims eventually go free; up to 90%.
- Escape if you can.
- Fight back immediately. The kidnapper is unlikely to kill you since their primary motivation is money. If the motivation is political rather than monetary, there is a good chance you will be killed anyway. Why not fight back? Statistically, the sooner you fight, the better the end result.

## Before You Return Home
Make sure you leave with everything you came with and do not leave any unpaid bills.

# 17
# TERRORISM

I debated whether to write a chapter on terrorism because there is an overwhelming amount of information available from multiple sources including FEMA, Homeland Security, the FBI and others. But to do so would be like ignoring the elephant in the room. The fact is that we have been involved in a global war on terror for almost a decade. It has put a huge strain on the deficit in the US and lives have been sacrificed fighting it. There has been a dramatic increase in terroristic acts during the last decade. Radical Muslims have overtly expressed their hatred of Jews and Israel, who are among the prominent players in the Middle East. Additionally, there are now an alarming number of domestic terrorists springing up. It is a fact of life. So are "spring uprisings", which have created significant instability in many foreign countries.

According to De Becker's research, when traveling abroad – where terrorism is more prevalent than in the United States;
- 71% of attacks come from multiple Adversaries and *not* the lone wolf.
- 71% of attacks come using firearms – with long guns (rifles) being used about 51% of the time and handguns used 20%.
- Most attacks in the US are less than 25 feet. This is true outside the US as well even though long guns are used more often. Creating space buffers of more than 25 feet almost guarantees the Principal's safety.
- IED's are much more popular outside the US. Bombs are about as successful as often as they fail. They fail 57% of the time. Attacks occur most frequently (64%) around the Principal's vehicle and are 77% successful. Therefore, the greatest single precaution that a Principal can take when outside of the United States is to travel in a fully armored car.

Although your Principal being caught up in terrorism may seem unlikely, you should have a working knowledge of terrorism if you travel internationally. Additionally, we are seeing more domestic terrorism acts now in the United States.

## Defined

Terrorism is a type of violent struggle that makes deliberate use of violence against civilians to achieve political aims. This is a struggle that is intended to harm public morale in which the terrorist organizations use all means available to them to carry out fatal attacks that will spread fear among a much wider population than those experiencing the attack. They intend to influence the public agenda and attract political and international attention to their ideological demands. By definition, terrorists want the biggest bang for their buck. They usually use IED's, suicide bombings or mass hostage taking in public gathering places to get someone's attention about something.

Terrorists have been known, however, to make targeted attacks against corporations and entities that do not share their values. Additionally, although kidnappings are rather rare in the United States, they do still happen – and more so overseas. For these reasons you should have a basic, functioning knowledge of terrorism. Terrorism is an international issue without borders. Different countries and movements around the world have found terrorism to be an effective means of advancing their political objectives. There are approximately 1.3 billion Muslims (people who practice Islam). Muslim birth rates are huge and the Islam faith is expected to overtake Christianity at some point, which sits at 2.3 billion. The Islamist terrorists are responsible for 98% of terrorism. Not everyone who practices Islam is a terrorist. Some Muslims believe in a complete separation of church and state. Others want expression through the established political system. There are Muslims who believe the world should operate through God's laws; not man's. It is a very small group of Muslims willing to use violence in order to achieve this. In the faith of Islam, a defensive war justifies any and all violence – even against women, children and other Muslims. Radical Muslims believe they are under attack from western values.

Jihad has several meanings:
- Personal: It is the internal struggle to be a better Muslim.
- Military: It is the external fight for Islam.
- Radical: There is no greater spiritual status than to die for this.

Young people are often recruited by radicals for the following reasons:
- Young people often push the envelope and are looking for thrills.

- They are easily influenced.
- They are looking for a sense of acceptance, belonging and family.

The Executive Summary from "American Jihadist Terrorism - Combating a Complex Threat", produced by the Congressional Research Service: "Between May 2009 and November 2010, arrests were made for 22 'homegrown', jihadist inspired terrorist plots by American citizens or legal permanent residents of the United States. By comparison, in more than seven years from the September 11, 2001 terrorist strikes through May 2009, there were 21 such plots. Two resulted in attacks, and no more than six plots occurred in a single year (2006). The apparent spike in such activity after May 2009 suggests that at least some Americans, even if a tiny minority, continue to be susceptible to ideologies supporting a violent form of jihad. This report describes homegrown violent jihadists and the plots and attacks that have occurred since 9/11. 'Homegrown' and 'domestic' are terms that describe terrorist activity or plots perpetrated within the United States or abroad by American citizens, legal permanent residents, or visitors radicalized largely within the United States. The term 'jihadist' describes radicalized individuals using Islam as an ideological and/or religious justification for their belief in the establishment of a global caliphate, or jurisdiction governed by a Muslim civil and religious leader known as a caliph. The term 'violent jihadist' characterizes jihadists who have made the jump to illegally supporting, plotting, or directly engaging in violent terrorist activity."

In 2008-2009 there was a significant increase in activity within the United States. Many people have questioned why the US has not had serious attacks since 9/11. A large part of that is due to governmental and law enforcement efforts to stop it. Over 22 plots have been thwarted in the US since 9/11 and over 60 in the United Kingdom. Terrorist sleeper cells have probably been in the US for years. It is probable and likely they have already studied and "cased" many soft targets. Making explosives is as simple as getting a recipe off of the Internet and then visiting your local hardware store. Why, then, have there not been suicide bombers and Improvised Explosive Devices exploding in the US? One of the primary reasons is the radical leadership behind terrorism is not stupid. They have not given sleeper cells the "green light". The US is a great place for foreigners to receive an excellent education, make good money to send back home, and operate freely in a republic. Why ruin a good thing?

## Methods of Terrorism

This section is a very general outline of terrorism and terrorist tactics. If you have more than a general interest in knowing what to look for and how to prepare, please visit the Homeland Security or FEMA website. As you read through this chapter, the overwhelming suggestion is that if you observe something that gets your attention, or speaks to your intuition, or causes a second look, or seems out of place or strange – something is probably not right, and you need to pay attention to it. What you do with that is entirely up to you, *but do not ignore it!*

## Conventional Terrorism

The Improvised Explosive Device is still the #1 weapon of choice for terrorists accounting for over 50% of all attacks.

Suspicious Object (Explosive Charge): A suspicious object is one that is unfamiliar and arouses suspicion due to its location because it has been placed there for the purpose of sabotage. If you come across a suspicious object, keep other people away from it and immediately inform authorities. One or more adults should watch over the suspicious object to make sure no one comes near while making sure they themselves are at a safe distance and if possible, behind a protective barrier.

Suspicious Person (Suicide Attack): A suicide attack is an "operational method in which the very act of the attack is dependent upon the death of the perpetrator." The terrorist is fully aware that if he does not kill himself, the planned attack will not be implemented. The attack is carried out by activating explosives worn or carried by the terrorist in the form of a portable explosive charge or planted in a vehicle he is driving. If you identify a suspicious person, keep him in sight and inform authorities. Try to prevent the suspect from approaching and/or entering any buildings.

From Terrorist Threat Indicators by Richard Marquis
Are unknown or suspicious people conducting boundary probing? They are checking to see how close they can get to the Target.
Wear heavy clothing to hide explosives regardless of the season, although there are now undergarments specifically made to hide explosive on the suicide bomber.
- Display a robotic gait or nervously look around.
- Show signs of tunnel vision and are not responsive to commands.
- Give the appearance of being drugged.
- Wear too much cologne or have other unusual smells.
- Carry a large backpack.

- Have wires protruding from sleeves or hands in pockets for detonation.
- Have a fresh shave or make other attempts to "blend in".
- Shows signs of emotion and irritation, or perspire excessively.
- Shows signs of being in clandestine collaboration and contact with other people directing signals and movements towards them.
- Appearance is unusual, does not suit their personality, or their clothes are not appropriate to the season.
- The suspect gives the impression that they may be concealing a weapon in their clothing.

Suspicious Vehicle (Car Bomb): If you discover a suspicious vehicle and none of the signs can be ruled out, it should be treated as if it is a weapon. Do not touch it or try to open the doors. Keep people away from the vehicle and close off access to the road. At the same time, inform the authorities about the vehicle and explain what has aroused your suspicion. A suspicious vehicle is one displaying one or more of the following signs:

- Suspicious or extra electric wires connected to the car.
- Additional electrical switches which appear suspicious.
- A safety catch in or near the vehicle.
- Torn pieces of insulating tape.
- A wrist watch, alarm clock or timer.
- Extraneous wires.
- Non-identical license plates.
- Absence of license plates.
- Signs of break-in indicating a stolen vehicle.
- Items or containers of flammable material inside the vehicle.
- A car parked in an unlikely and suspicious manner.
- A vehicle that appears to be low due to excessive weight.

## Non-Conventional Terrorism

These tactics involve the use of a non-conventional component (atomic, biological or chemical) and is therefore likely to cause more serious damage to the surrounding area, affecting water or food, or causing disease in people, animals or plants. The use of conventional terrorism can sometimes lead to a non-conventional incident such as rockets fired at a plant containing hazardous materials. This then becomes a hazardous materials incident.

Suspicious Packages and Letters: Be wary of suspicious packages and letters. They may contain explosives, chemical or biological agents. Be particularly cautious at your place of employment. Some typical characteristics postal inspectors have detected over the years which ought to trigger suspicion include parcels that:

- Are unexpected or from someone unfamiliar to you.
- Have no return address, or have one that can't be verified as legitimate.
- Have protruding wires or aluminum foil, strange odors, or stains.
- Show a city or state in the postmark that doesn't match the return address.
- Are of unusual weight given their size, or are lopsided or oddly shaped.
- Are marked with threatening language.
- Have inappropriate or unusual labeling.
- Have excessive postage or packaging material such as masking tape and string.
- Have misspellings of common words.
- Are addressed to someone no longer with your organization or are otherwise outdated.
- Have incorrect titles or titles without a name.
- Are not addressed to a specific person.
- Have hand-written or poorly typed addresses.

With suspicious envelopes and packages other than those that might contain explosives, take these additional steps against possible biological and chemical agents.

- Refrain from eating or drinking in a designated mail handling area.
- Place suspicious envelopes or packages in a plastic bag or some other type of container to prevent leakage of contents. Never sniff or smell suspect mail.
- If you do not have a container, then cover the envelope or package with anything available (e.g., clothing, paper, trash can, etc.) and do not remove the cover.
- Leave the room and close the door or section off the area to prevent others from entering.
- Wash your hands with soap and water to prevent spreading any substance to your face.
- If you are at work, report the incident to your building security official or supervisor who should notify police and other authorities without delay.
- List all people who were in the room or area when this suspicious letter or package was recognized. Give a copy of this list to both the

local public health authorities and law enforcement officials for follow-up investigations and advice.

- If you are at home, report the incident to local police.

*Biological agents* are organisms or toxins that can kill or incapacitate people, livestock, and crops. The three basic groups of biological agents that would likely be used as weapons are bacteria, viruses, and toxins. Most biological agents are difficult to grow and maintain. Many break down quickly when exposed to sunlight and other environmental factors, while others, such as anthrax spores, are very long lived. Biological agents can be dispersed by spraying them into the air, by infecting animals that will carry the disease to humans and by contaminating food and water.

*Chemical agents* are poisonous vapors, aerosols, liquids, and solids that have toxic effects on people, animals, or plants. They can be released by bombs or sprayed from aircraft, boats, and vehicles. They can be used as a liquid to create a hazard to people and the environment. Some chemical agents may be odorless and tasteless. They can have an immediate effect (a few seconds to a few minutes) or a delayed effect (2 to 48 hours). While potentially lethal, chemical agents are difficult to deliver in lethal concentrations. Outdoors, the agents often dissipate rapidly. Chemical agents also are difficult to produce. A chemical attack could come without warning. Signs of a chemical release include people having difficulty breathing; experiencing eye irritation; losing coordination; becoming nauseated; or having a burning sensation in the nose, throat, and lungs. Also, the presence of many dead insects or birds may indicate a chemical agent release.

*A nuclear blast* is an explosion with intense light and heat, a damaging pressure wave, and widespread radioactive material that can contaminate the air, water, and ground surfaces for miles around. A nuclear device can range from a weapon carried by an intercontinental missile launched by a hostile nation or terrorist organization to a small portable nuclear device transported by an individual. All nuclear devices cause deadly effects when they explode including blinding light, intense heat, nuclear radiation, blast effects, fires started by the heat pulse and secondary fires caused by the destruction. The extent, nature, and arrival time of these hazards are difficult to predict. Geographical dispersion of hazard effects will be defined by the size of the device, the height at detonation, the nature of the surface beneath the explosion and existing meteorological conditions. Even if individuals are not close enough to the nuclear blast to be affected by the direct impacts, they may be affected by radioactive fallout. Any nuclear blast results in some fallout. Blasts that occur near the earth's surface create much greater amounts of fallout than blasts that occur at higher altitudes. This is because the tremendous heat produced from a nuclear blast causes an up-draft of air that forms the familiar mushroom cloud. When a blast occurs near the earth's surface, millions of vaporized dirt particles also are drawn into the cloud. As the heat diminishes, radioactive materials that have vaporized condense on the particles and fall back to Earth. The phenomenon is called radioactive fallout. This fallout material decays over a long period of time and is the main source of residual nuclear radiation.

In addition to other effects, a nuclear weapon detonated in or above the earth's atmosphere can create an *electromagnetic pulse* (EMP), which is a high-density electrical field. An EMP acts like a stroke of lightning but is stronger, faster, and shorter. An EMP can seriously damage electronic devices connected to power sources or antennas. This includes communication systems, computers, electrical appliances, and automobile or aircraft ignition systems. The damage could range from a minor interruption to actual burnout of components. Most electronic equipment within 1,000 miles of a high-altitude nuclear detonation could be affected. Battery-powered radios with short antennas generally would not be affected. Although an EMP is unlikely to harm most people, it could harm those with pacemakers or other implanted electronic devices.

In general, potential targets for these weapons include:
- Strategic missile sites and military bases.
- Centers of government such as Washington, DC and state capitals.
- Important transportation and communication centers.
- Manufacturing, industrial, technology, and financial centers.
- Petroleum refineries, electrical power plants, and chemical plants.
- Major ports and airfields.

A *Radiological Dispersion Device* (RDD), often called "dirty nuke" or "dirty bomb", is considered far more likely than use of a nuclear explosive device. An RDD combines a conventional explosive device, such as a bomb, with radioactive material. It is designed to scatter dangerous and sub-lethal amounts of radioactive material over a general area. Such RDDs appeal to terrorists because they require limited technical knowledge to build and deploy compared to a nuclear device. Also, the radioactive materials in RDDs are widely used in medicine, agriculture, industry, and research and are easier to obtain than weapons grade uranium or plutonium. The primary purpose of terrorist use of an RDD is to cause psychological fear and economic disruption. Some devices could cause fatalities from exposure to radioactive materials. Depending on the speed at which the area of the RDD detonation was evacuated or how successful people were at sheltering-in-place, the number of deaths and injuries from an RDD might not be substantially greater than from a conventional bomb explosion. The size of the affected area and the level of destruction caused by an RDD would depend on the sophistication and size of the conventional bomb, the type of radioactive material used, the quality and quantity of the radioactive material, and the local meteorological conditions; primarily wind and precipitation. The area affected could be placed off-limits to the public for several months during cleanup efforts.

## What Can Be Done to Fight Suicide Terrorism?

Individuals and organizations that are concerned about being a target of terror should be conducting protective intelligence, practicing operational counter-terrorist measures and protective antiterrorist measures. Psychological measures should be employed to whatever degree is possible. Operational (counter-terrorist) measures are efforts towards putting pressure on those elements involved in the overall planning and implementation of attacks.

Security Measures (anti-terrorist measures) should be taken in order to prevent the Adversary from reaching his Target or getting inside the Target. Psychological Measures has to do with countering the moral damage of these attacks. Of foremost importance is the task of supporting and strengthening the civilian population in dealing with suicide terrorism. Civilians are the main victims of terrorism and it is they who are on the front line in the fight against terrorism.

## The Tell

There is, almost always, a precursor, or "tell" before a terror attack. Much like Mass Shooters, the terrorist leaves a trail of things that are often missed by officials and the public.

- Parking or loitering in the same area over a period of days, with no apparent reason.
- Cameras or video cameras with special magnification lenses or night vision devices.
- Photos, maps, sketches, or blueprints of potential targets.
- Computer access to information about sensitive sites, such as nuclear plants.
- Unusual false alarms requiring law enforcement or emergency response.
- Evidence of coded communication.
- Books and pamphlets promoting Jihad.
- Bomb-making manuals.

- Flight manuals.
- Logs or records detailing the activities or movements of law enforcement or security personnel.
- Thefts at military surplus stores.
- Rental of storage units.
- Modification of vehicles, including trucks and limousines, to accommodate heavy loads.
- Access to emergency vehicles.
- Signs of training and testing.
- Possession or attempts to acquire ammonium nitrate fertilizer, body armor, propane bottles and tanks, uniforms, identification, license plates, service vehicles, weapons, ammunition, chemicals, identification documents, prepaid cell phones, and ATM cards.
- Funding sources include counterfeit designer clothing & jewelry, drugs, money laundering, smuggling, stolen property, sales of publications and fraud.

Domestic Terror warning signs include radical bumper stickers, homemade or missing license plates, fraudulent driver's license or registrations, message-tattoos, video surveillance on property, weapons, ammunition or explosives and possession of radical literature. The average terrorist does not look like one. They look like all of us. Therefore, profiling based on race, gender and looks is futile. Profiling should be done, and it should be based on the behavioral indicators already mentioned. Additionally, if you are ever caught up in a terror event you have two choices and must make them quickly. Flee immediately if you can. If not, you must fight and do it quickly. Case study after case study reveals the longer you wait to respond, the worse things are going to get. A terroristic act needs to be met with a violent counterattack immediately.

## Taking It To The Next Level

You can use these same principles to deter terrorism and reduce risk to your Asset.

There have been a number of terror incidents both in the United States and abroad in which innocent civilians have found themselves in situations from which they could not escape. These include school shootings, mall shootings, mass transit attacks, workplace violence incidents and hostage-taking. Think about them and consider what immediate actions you would take in these situations if you were present with your Principal.

List 3 proactive steps that every agent or team should be taking in relation to discovering the potential Terrorist.

In regard to what you have read in this chapter, list three specific things that you might observe which would cause you to take some course of action with your Principal – whether that be evasive action or planning differently.

# 18
# THE ONLY EXECUTIVE PROTECTION CHECKLIST YOU WILL EVER NEED

It is helpful to take the team approach to planning and coordinating protection events and assignments. The core components of this book are biased towards the Executive Safety professional who might be in a supervisory or planning role. It was written this way with purpose. If you understand the Executive Safety function from the viewpoint of a person who carries great responsibility for its outcome - your overall expertise as an Executive Safety professional will be greatly enhanced.

I understand many VIP/Executive Protection courses and schools emphasize specific post assignments and skills. The result is an Agent who may excel in specific post tactics but does not have the ability to see the big picture. I want you to be able to understand all of the components of Executive Safety in hopes that you will become a well-rounded Executive Safety professional.

What follows in this chapter are the chronological tasks leading up to a protection detail or event. This checklist includes meetings that might take place as you work through the tasks. Please adapt the checklist to suit your particular event or detail.

I understand you may not be required to participate in any of these functions, particularly if you are part of a team where you are an Agent assigned to a particular post position with very specific post orders. However, you may be called upon to provide input at any given time, in any given area. And some day you may find yourself in a supervisory position or owning your own company.

## Legal

- Do I need to be operating under a license in this state?
- Is this detail or event armed or unarmed?
- What are the Use of Force laws & regulations?
- Are my Agents trained in Use of Force?

## Defining The Mission & Key Components

- What is the Mission?
- Are the Critical Assets defined?
- Have I completed an Asset Survey?
- Do I have or need an Itinerary?
- Do I have or need an Event Schedule?
- Have I defined the Primary Threats?
- Have I defined an Adversary?
- If so, have I defined the likely Adversary's motivation and goals?
- If so, have I defined the likely Method of Operation?
- Have I conducted Protective Intelligence?

## Targets & Mitigation

- Have Targets been identified?
- Have I completed a prioritized list of Targets?
- When doing so, have I considered transportation, airport, and hotels?
- Have I conducted a Site Advance Field Work?
- When Site Advance Work was completed did I define Inner, Middle & Outer Perimeters?
- Have I assigned Risk Scores to the vulnerabilities discovered at each Target?
- Have I considered Undesirable Consequences?
- Have I collected relevant Policies & Procedures?
- Do I need to develop my own policies and procedures, or contingency plans for my Agents or for this event?
- Have I mitigated discovered Risks through changes in Policies or using Physical Barriers, Technology & People?
- What technical or logistical support is needed?
- Should I subcontract this or do I need to provide it?
- Are there outside resources available that can be of assistance?
- How many Agents do I need?
- Have I organized all of this Threat information?

## Assigning Posts

- Have I considered General Emergencies?
- Have I assigned a Command Post?
- Have I assigned Post positions?
- Have I created Post Orders?
- Are the Agents I assign to Posts trained to carry out the responsibilities specific to that Post?

## Final Countdown to the Event

Have I gathered relevant information and conducted specialized meetings that have considered or addressed the following?

- Intelligence
- Surveillance
- Transportation
- Safe & Relocation Zones
- Emergency Planning
- Site Security
- Inner Perimeter
- Specialized Support Elements

## Communication Before the Event

- Have I updated schedules and intelligence?
- Have final plans been published or released?
- Have I met regularly with the key players on my team?
- Does everyone know what they are doing and what is expected of them? Clear communication of this is critical to excellent performance.

# 19
# ASSESSING & MANAGING VIOLENT BEHAVIOR

There have been volumes written over the years regarding violence and violent behavior. For our purposes we need to consider all that great research and information, but we also need to condense it into easily understood principles that the average person can assimilate without dedicating years studying it.

Violence and violent behavior have been around since the beginning of time. There are forms of violence which are generally justified. Very few people would argue that the shopping mall, church, workplace or school campus shooter needs to be neutralized – with lethal force if necessary. Additionally, there have been bloody wars that have taken place in the name of human rights that most people would agree are justified. There are other forms of violent behavior in which we look at the violent person and can only ascribe their actions to evil. How do we come to grips with the violence human beings perpetrate upon each other?

In order to understand violence and violent behavior, you must, to some degree, put yourself in the mindset of the violent person; whatever that mindset may be. If you attempt to understand violent behavior from your own frame of reference, it makes no sense......unless your frame of reference includes the study or personal experience of violence.

Example: there are people who view alcoholism or drug abuse as a matter of personal discipline or will; mind over matter. This is ignorant thinking. You would be hard pressed to find a recovering alcoholic who shares this view. Addictive personality traits, urges and the feelings of personal bondage is something the person in recovery can relate to. The recovering alcoholic understands the alcoholic's abusive behavior, deceit and manipulative behavior that comes with "using". A person who has no frame of reference to understand the alcoholic creates their own understanding of the behavior. In the same context, there are violent behaviors that seem to be perfectly rational choices for the violent person, based on the root causes of the behavior. Bottom line: lack of education and information creates a vacuum in which people "fill in the blanks" to understand anything they wonder about. The mind simply makes things up. It is how our brains work.

Herein lays the importance of studying violence. An empirical (as defined by appropriate observation and experimentation) understanding of violent people and violent behavior will give you a foundational frame of reference that will allow you to assess and manage violence when it presents itself.

## What We Know About Violent Crime

Violent crime includes murder, rape and sexual assault, robbery, and assault.

- Violence, in its various forms, is considered a public health problem by the Center for Disease Control.
- Over the course of a year, over 7 million people are directly affected by the consequences of violent acts.
- 20 of every 100,000 people in the United States will be a victim of violent crime. This is significantly higher than England, Germany or Switzerland. These figures change significantly depending on what data base you use as a reference.
- 8 of every 100,000 will be a homicide victim. Since 2000, this rate has been stable.
- In the last 10 years there has been a 17% decline in violent crime.
- You are far more likely to be the victim of a robbery than an assault with injury or sexual assault. However, robberies have violent characteristics.
- The average duration of a typical violent encounter is less than 2 minutes. The average police response time in the US is 6 minutes and 50 seconds.
- In 24% of the incidents of violent crime, a weapon was present.
- Homicides are most often committed with guns, especially handguns. In 2005, 55% of homicides were committed with handguns, 16% with other guns, 14% with knives, 5% with blunt objects, and 11% with other weapons.
- An examination of the 2004 supplemental data regarding the type of weapons offenders used in the commission of the robbery revealed that assailants relied on strong-arm tactics in 41.1 percent of robberies during 2004; they employed firearms in 40.6 percent of robberies. Offenders used knives or other cutting instruments in 8.9

percent of these crimes. In the remaining 9.4 percent of robberies, the offenders used other types of weapons.

- Offenders had or used a weapon in 48% of all robberies, compared with 22% of all aggravated assaults.
- There are approximately 350,000 churches in the United States. There are approximately 22 incidents a year (average 10 years based on data from page 7 – which is incomplete). Based on these statistics, there is a .006 % chance of one of these incidents occurring in your church.
- The chance of being a victim of violent crime if you live in the United States is 1-2%.

## Violence Categories
- Premeditated or learned violence.
- Medically related violence – secondary to illness: closed head injuries, panic attacks, thought disorders, neurological disorders.
- Impulsive violence is un-thought out, unregulated, and a violent emotional response. Incoming information is not processed properly, and there is a lack of inhibitory controls. There are few reflective, moderating experiences that impulsive people draw from – presumably because they process incoming information poorly (described below). They also seem to lack the self-control to refrain from repeating this behavior.

Impulsive people tend to develop psychiatric problems, become substance abusers and are characteristic of anti-social personality disorder. Normal inhibitions that most of us have get no time to rise up within these people.
Their internal inhibitions say: "I am not responsible for my life." Their external inhibitions say: "I have no control; my life is ruled by external events." The need to satisfy immediate needs is all they focus on. The way to diffuse this is by keeping them in the here and now, not yesterday or tomorrow.

A violent person's behavior may have roots in all three categories, with most stemming from two categories.

## Violent Behavior

- Violence is a rare event and developing baseline behavior is difficult.
- The yearly occurrence within a normal population is 2.75% for males and 1% for females.
- Not everyone is violent all the time. Most people have internal blocks or inhibitions that prevent them from acting out in a violent manner, even when they experience situations that might otherwise lead to a violent response.
- Of those incarcerated and released as "potentially violent", 25-30% are re-arrested.

## How Most People Are Wired

People are not complex. Perception precedes Thought. Thought precedes Impulse. Impulse precedes Action. This is why perception is incredibly important. It is where Action begins to form. **Perception Is Everything!** Perception occurs on a conscious and unconscious level. Read the Adversary. They are reading you. How do they perceive you? How do they perceive the circumstances? What is their perception of you?

- Anger is neither necessary nor sufficient to produce violent behavior.
- Anger can be an appropriate emotional response, whereas aggression is not. The difference between the two is that aggression generally involves physical action that precedes violence. Aggressive action is a response to fear. Anger is okay. If a person is allowed to vent anger without endangering anyone, the risk of violence can be reduced tremendously. Anger example: A subject is pacing back and forth, swearing and screaming. Aggression involves physically threatening behavior. Aggression example: after throwing an object against a wall, the person rapidly approaches you and gets in your face; swearing.
- Acting out violently, on anger, is the result of the absence of behavior problem solving skills.

Verbal aggression is an attempt to assert dominance or control – the human form of animal threat displays. There are also aggressive behaviors that are often precursors to violent behavior. If you observe these behaviors, they are red flags and your guard should go up – although they do not guarantee violence. They are:

- Conspicuously Ignoring: this is the person that is looking around or seemingly occupied with something else while you are attempting to engage or direct them. They act as if you are not there.

- Exaggerated Attention: this is the person who is asking way too many questions or seems to be inappropriately concerned about what you are doing.
- Excited Movement: This is the person who is throwing things around, furiously pacing, wildly swinging their arms around, etc.
- Attack.

## How Most Violent People Are Wired

Extremely assaultive people tend to be over-controlled and use the unconscious defenses of:

- Repression: the exclusion of distressing memories, thoughts, or feelings from the conscious mind. Often involving sexual or aggressive urges or painful childhood memories, these unwanted mental contents are pushed into the unconscious mind. Repression is thought to give rise to anxiety and to neurotic symptoms, which begin when a forbidden drive or impulse threatens to enter the conscious mind.
- Denial: Denial is the refusal to acknowledge the existence or severity of unpleasant external realities or internal thoughts and feelings.
- Displacement: a subconscious defense mechanism whereby the mind redirects affects from an object felt to be dangerous or unacceptable to an object felt to be safe or acceptable. For instance, some people punch cushions when angry at friends; a college student may snap at his or her roommate when upset about an exam grade.
- Sublimation: sublimation is a coping mechanism. It is the refocusing of psychic energy away from negative outlets to more positive outlets. These drives which cannot find an outlet are rechanneled. For example, a student who has a major upcoming test, rather than spending time and energy worrying about it, might re-channel that time and energy into studying; and a person full of rage who is accustomed to wasting time and energy on lashing out at others, might instead re-channel those outlets towards expressions of art, music or poetry.

The key to recognizing defensive and irrational behavior – which has potential to become violent - is "appropriateness". When you see behavior that seems inappropriate, you should be analyzing what is really going on.

Irrational anger and assaultive behavior is generally associated with schizophrenia, organic brain syndrome, alcoholism, drug abuse and to a lesser degree: hormones & adolescence.

"It's all about me!" Violent, aggressive people tend to be arrogant, conceited, egotistical, narcissistic, or otherwise enamored with who they are. People who have a high opinion of themselves tend to react irrationally, impulsively and emotionally when something presents a serious challenge to these favorable views. *When this balloon is pricked – they explode.*

## The Nature of Conflict
When the goals of two or more people are opposed conflict will exist. Conflict occurs in two modes: verbal and physical. The strength of conflict depends on the will of each party. People engage in conflicts in which they have no chance of winning because of emotion, not logic. Emotion drives behavior. Here we are, back to that perception thing again – because a person's perception is going to drive their thoughts, which in turn affects emotion. Understanding the emotional roots of the conflict is the key to controlling it. If you can "tap" into the emotion driving the behavior, you have a better chance of de-fusing it. Women are generally better at this than men. Expect to be uncomfortable, because the person presenting the conflict is setting the tone; not you.

## Brain Disorders & Mental Illness
Irrational anger and assaultive behavior is generally associated with schizophrenia, organic brain syndrome and alcoholism.

Mental illness appears only rarely to play a key role in violent behavior, unless substance abuse is involved.

Functionally mentally ill people are 5 times less dangerous than the normal population with the exception of bipolars, schizophrenics and acute psychosis.

There is growing evidence that among murderer's brain defects is the rule, not the exception. Brain damage "clearly characterizes the extremely violent." Reducing stimulation reduces aggression in brain damaged people.

There are Emotionally Disturbed People (EDP's) who are human powder kegs. They are withdrawn from reality, fearful and potentially violent. They resent and fear authority. They have a distorted self-image and possess the ability to change behavior rapidly. They carry feelings of defensiveness-suspicion-persecution and are often delusional. Never underestimate their intelligence.

## Predicting Violence

Psychological testing cannot predict violent behavior. Violence prediction evaluation must include habit strength, motivational factors, situational factors and inhibition factors. There are specific evaluations and assessments used to predict different types of violence. Non-mental health professionals are as accurate in predicting violent behavior if they use the same criteria. Past violence is the best predictor of future violence! Look at the historical data. Variables which increase the chance for violence:

- Psychiatric involvement: 2-12%
- Marijuana: 19%
- Alcohol: 25%
- Other drugs: 35%

A combination of two or more of the above doubles the chance for violence.

## What to Do About the Potentially Violent Person

You have a job to do. Just do it – professionally and with direct compassion. What the subject does is not your fault. If things fall apart, you are not responsible for another's behavior. You can, however, shape and influence behavior by applying these principles.

In a crisis you may lose up to 70% of your verbal and physical skills. This is disturbing. When you need these skills the most, they are not available. The Fight or Flight Syndrome reactions you have little control over include shaking, blood pressure, muscle twitching and tenseness, epinephrine released from the adrenal glands – adrenaline, loss of blood to brain, ability to think and make cognitive decisions, time distortion, loss of physical and verbal skills, auditory changes and memory loss among other things.

Your values, self-concept, conditioning, previous job experience and training will dictate your response. *Be professional.* Fear is good. Panic is not. Do not over or under react. Violence is reduced when we display extraordinary levels of professionalism, human compassion, common sense and sound judgment. The only thing that will help you prepare for this is practicing techniques, mental imaging and simulations through training. Once an incident begins, you should breathe slow and self-talk.

In a study of officer related assaults, 75% of officers added to the problem, contributed mostly by body language and words.

Use clear communication. The person will do what they want to do unless convinced or forced to do otherwise. You need to control the person's choices. Remember, the exchange may be insulting, but its business – not personal. People want to be heard. Listen. Ask leading questions and encourage ventilation. Try to see the issue from their side to figure out the emotional roots of the conflict. Do not be judgmental. Do not abuse or threaten. Don't leave anything to assumption. If you do, in the space of that vacuum, the person will create his or her own information.

- Use persuasion: "It will be in your best interest to comply because if you do not there may be unpleasant consequences that really are not necessary."
- Use advice: "It might be better if we seek to resolve this by ........."
- Warning: "It is unfortunate that we cannot go on with this any longer. If you do not comply, I will have to......."
- Enforce the warning.
- Do not promise anything you cannot deliver.

Conversely, your Adversary will automatically try to manipulate you and take advantage by:

- Your weaknesses.
- Technical arguments.
- The environment.
- Attack or escape.

Get help. Do not try to handle it alone: 2 people present reduce the risk of violence by 80+% and 3 people present – up to 95%.

Distance: give them plenty of it. Most people get more anxious when their "space bubble" is violated.

Atmosphere: Resist the impulse to do something immediately. Attempt to stabilize the situation and slow things down. Do you really have to take action now? Take your time and talk. Try to calm the person. Convey an image of quiet self assurance. Statistically, allowing a 3-minute vent reduces the chance of violence to almost zero, and the real problem will come out. But to do so you must try to discover the underlying emotional root. Try to identify and label emotions and feelings you are hearing.

Remember, the surest predictor of whether an individual will use violent behavior to obtain what they want or to resolve a grievance is to determine if they have used violence for such purposes in the past.

Keep a safe distance of 4-6 feet; a two-arm length minimum. When you invade this buffer zone the person will become more anxious. Play TAG if the person becomes physically active and begins to move around.

Look for escape routes. Be ready to disengage or use force. If force becomes necessary apply with 100% intent and move quickly.

The extent to which a subject is able to carry out an attack requires a weapon, a victim and foiling any security measures.

Final note: people wonder if it is okay to deceive and lie to the potential Adversary. Generally speaking, you should not deceive. However, be aware that deceit can be an effective tactic under certain conditions.

## Body Language
The clues to people's real intentions are:
- Verbal Content is 7-10% of true intent.  People Lie.
- Voice: Listen to the pace, pitch, tone and modulation. This will reveal 33-40% of true intent.
- Non-Verbal Body Language: Body Motion, Posture, Distance, Movement, Stance and HANDS will reveal 50-60% of true intent.

Positive Body Language
- Leaning forward
- Touching neck
- Standing with one hand on hip
- Hands clasped together

Defensive Positions
- Crossing arms or legs
- Fidgeting or toe-tapping
- Doodling
- Touching hair or face
- Wrinkling nose which raises the top lip
- Shifting from foot to foot
- Hands behind back
- Rubbing back of head

Signals Someone is Lying
- Lack of eye contact
- Sweating
- Excessive hand movements
- Ears turn red
- Shifting in seat or shifting while standing

<u>Signs of the Possibility of Pending Aggression</u>
- Red-faced or white-faced / Sweating
- Pacing, restless, or repetitive movements; violating your personal space
- Trembling or shaking / Clenched jaws or fists
- Exaggerated or violent gestures
- Change in voice, Loud talking or chanting
- Shallow, rapid breathing
- Scowling, sneering or use of abusive language
- Glaring or avoiding eye contact

**The Characteristics of an Armed Person**
The 2 most common traits of a person who is carrying a weapon are their physical appearance and behavior. We know statistically that guns, knives and blunt objects are the weapons most often used in violent crime. Most weapons are hidden from view until the Adversary intends to use them. HANDS are required to operate a weapon and initiate an attack. Watch the hands!

Look for the following indicators:
- Will touch or adjust area of weapon placement.
- Jacket pocket will sag due to weight of weapon.
- Warm long jacket worn in warm weather.
- Wearing only one glove on cold day.
- Observe bulge in pocket of pants, side of pants or back of pants.
- Unnatural walks or gate. May limp or hold leg when walking. Bulge in pant leg.
- Run with hand on pocket or leg side due to holding weapon in place.
- Hesitate when asked to comply.
- Back away as you approach.
- Keep arm against body.
- Stand with strong side back in bladed position.

<u>Inside of Vehicle Watch For</u>
- Shoulder drops or head movement upon approach.
- May re-adjust areas of body were weapon is held.

**Approaching the Potential Armed Adversary**
If possible approach from the rear side. Approaching from the rear makes it more difficult for them to draw their weapon, aim and shoot accurately. 85%

of them are right-handed and have to swing across or turn around to shoot. This buys you some reaction time.

**A Final Word About Weapons for the Executive Protection Agent**
Just about every EP Agent I have ever met is always "on". They are naturally aware of their surroundings and always processing the environment, people and circumstances through the eyes of a protective warrior, even when they are not on assignment.

How far do you need you need to go in terms of preparation?

Mass shootings, workplace violence and other sensational crimes of violence seem to surround us through media coverage. What do you really need for personal self-defense? Do you need to enroll in a martial arts course and obtain a $5,000.00 black belt? Become an expert sharpshooter? Booby-trap the yard?

I take a holistic approach toward personal protection, corporate safety and self-defense. Three elements come into play with *any* unexpected emergency – and they deeply affect the outcome.

- *Cognitive ability:* This is the intellectual ability, or thinking process which includes planning, tactics and decision-making. Cognitive skills increase through learning, study and discussion.
- *Affective skills:* The ability to control psychological reactions under stress is largely determined by the degree of emotional stability, practical experience and spiritual maturity a person possesses.
- *Motor skills:* Does the person experiencing the emergency know the appropriate response? Have they been trained in the use of appropriate physical actions? Do they have appropriate weapons or tools to effectively deal with the situation or incident?

Here is what you really need to protect yourself, your loved ones, your organization, your community or your Principal. Decide which ones makes sense in your daily environment.

Purchase the products and learn how to use them. By doing so you are increasing your motor skills and building an appropriate Toolbox for unexpected violent behavior and other emergencies.

Read as much as you can. Knowledge is power. Nurture your skills.

## Firearms

Statistically, it is highly unlikely you will ever pull your handgun out and point it at someone, much less pull the trigger. You are far more likely to use less-than-lethal options. Outside of Castle Doctrine states, generally, you have no legal right in any state to take a life unless they are presenting a threat that will result in great bodily injury or death. Being prepared for the worst is always a good idea and we fully endorse handgun ownership. However, we also encourage you to prepare for that which is statistically much more likely.

Purchase a firearm along with a legal permit and determine a method of carrying it. Use it to defend yourself or someone else if your perception is that death (or in some states – serious or great bodily harm) will result from what you see taking place. Don't worry too much about the caliber. If you hit someone with a bullet it is going to hurt them, allowing you to escape or evacuate your Principal.

Research clearly indicates stopping power has more to do with the manufacture of the bullet, not necessarily the caliber. Buy a handgun that fits your hand very comfortably and one you can shoot well with.

A shotgun, although not necessary, is a good idea for home defense. The Remington 870 and Mossberg 500 models have been around a long time and are reasonably priced.

A Firearm is not the total solution to the problem. Avoiding the problem is safer!

### Firearm Defense Facts

- 40% of those shot in the heart will survive.
- If shot in the heart a person may still fight for over one minute.
- 85% or more of self-defense shootings are in low light or darkness.
- 90% or more will be at 21 feet or less, most are 10 feet or less.
- If you are shot in the chest with a handgun, your chance of dying is 14%.
- If you are shot twice, your chances of dying are 70%.
- If shot in the chest with an AK-47, the odds of death are 17%, with a shotgun; 64%.

### Pepper Spray, Tasers & Stun Guns

Always check your state statutes and local ordinances for any restrictions or requirements when purchasing or possessing any of these weapons. Use these weapons only after reviewing them thoroughly. Although not necessary, it is preferable you take a class and receive certification in any weapon you carry or intend to use. This will insure that you use it properly and reduce liability in the event that you do have to use it. Pepper Spray is best used between 3 & 15 feet. This allows you to avoid direct contact with an Adversary. The same principle applies to the Taser, unless you miss your target when you shoot. The Stun Gun requires direct contact with the Adversary. Stun Guns and Taser use different technologies.

Control Instruments
These are typically a long, hard, cylindrical object and are used to create tremendous pain on different pressure sensitive areas of the Adversary's body. Typically, you would use a control instrument only if you cannot escape and the Adversary has grabbed you or your Principal.

You might also use it to assist another person who is being attacked. I suggest you consider combining the Pepper Spray and the Control Instrument by purchasing the ASP Key Defender. This is my #1 recommendation for a defensive weapon. It combines a key strike (which is a type of impact weapon) along with a control instrument (kubaton) and pepper spray which is easily released. There is a safety mechanism for the pepper spray to reduce the risk of accidental discharge.

Impact Weapon & Flashlights
An impact weapon is used to create impact (not pressure) on an area of the body. Classic impact weapons are batons or flashlights. These are very effective if you need to strike an Adversary. Target areas are the arms and legs and shoulders. Use an impact instrument only if the Adversary is within appropriate striking distance.

Flashlights are not only used for emergency lighting when you need it. When a flashlight is unexpectedly aimed at an Adversary's eyes, it will temporary disrupt their vision allowing you to escape. The bulb (measured in lumens) needs to be bright enough to have this effect.

Purchase a flashlight that is bright enough to disrupt an Adversary's sight and has a bezel on the end. This allows you to use it as an effective impact weapon or control instrument if needed. As an example, Smith & Wesson makes a fine choice of tactical flashlights.

Knives
A good self-defense knife will be a spring assist folding knife with a blade made of tough, durable steel, such as ATS-34, ATS-55, and AUS-6. Look for a handle and grip that is comfortable, can be held securely and has finger and

thumb protection. Practice. Conceal it in a place where you can retrieve it and engage it quickly.

**Note:** For any weapon to be effective, it needs to be with you and retrievable in a quick manner.

# ABOUT THE AUTHOR

- Terry Hipp is a career veteran of the Criminal Justice System and the Private Security Industry. He serves as the CEO and Sr. Director of Training & Education at Assault Prevention LLC (AssaultPrevention.Org)

- Assault Prevention helps individuals, groups, and organizations proactively plan for successful mitigation of unexpected violence and emergencies through assessments, consultation, training & instruction and social media. This includes corporate threat assessment of physical facilities, intellectual property, and key personnel; specialized security and presentation of local, national, and global trend research and analysis.

- Assault Prevention has provided consultation, instruction and customized training to 100+ Federal, State and Local Criminal Justice Agencies, and 50+ private and non-profit organizations.

- Previously he served in a variety of roles within Institutional Corrections, Law Enforcement, Community Corrections and Private Security including Detective, Narcotics & Vice, SWAT, Bomb Squad Member, Arson Investigator, State Emergency Response & Planning Team Member, Instructor, Research Analyst, Fugitive Apprehension and VIP Protection.

- He provides certified instruction in Use of Force, Executive Safety, Firearms, Personal Protection, Risk Management, and Threat Assessment & Planning.

- His certifications include Senior Control Tactics Instructor, Master Handgun Instructor, Lethal Force Training Master Instructor, Certified Personal Protection Specialist, NRA Certified Pistol Instructor, MN DNR Certified Firearms Safety Instructor, Risk Assessment & Threat Management Specialist and is a Validated Expert in Community Vulnerability Assessments.

- He has developed curriculums and has authored articles and books, including <u>Last Call: Picking Up the Sword of the Spirit</u>, and <u>Feel Safe?</u>

Made in the USA
Lexington, KY
04 March 2014